The Night's Magician:
Poems about the Moon

PRAISE FOR *THE NIGHT'S MAGICIAN*

In this anthology of poems, 80 gifted contributors from Baltimore to Bucharest reacquaint us with the luminous, numinous moon—and what a delightful meeting it is! As I sit listening to Holst's *The Planets,* feasting my eyes on this printed panorama of moonstruck mindscapes, the irony of this strange Black Moon month when our astral partner hides from our view is impressed upon me as I write, and I am reminded how much I miss her. Sue Walker and Philip Kolin have skillfully brought this collection together, giving readers welcome respite from the burdens of the earthly mundane. Whether profoundly thoughtful or playfully humorous, each poem lodges itself cozily within the reader. No one should deny themselves the pleasures of this lunar mosaic.

>   —Michael A. Flannery, Professor Emeritus of UAB Libraries, and author of *Nature's Prophet: Alfred Russel Wallace's Evolution from Natural Selection to Natural Theology*

Let me tell the honest-to-moon truth. This collection makes me feel kin to everybody—Stuart, Maria, William, Lou Ella, Robert, Karen, Joseph, Marley, Peter, Linda—and on: everyone inside and outside its radius. After all, haven't we all shared the moon? Hasn't it accompanied us all, through everything? My own favorite has been the gibbous moon, the curve of its back resembling an ape; a shape I can feel not-too-distantly related to—way out there. This is a collection that brings us all closer together—a magical anthology.

>   —Sena Jeter Naslund, author of *Four Spirits; Ahab's Wife; Adam & Eve; The Fountain of St. James Court,* or *Portrait of the Artist as an Old Woman*

This anthology is a striking poetic counterpart of the moon's nocturnal magic. Projecting upward their questioning, their awe, fantasy, and visions, word-magicians display here their sleight-of-hand with the light and shadow of substance and form. Although free association is often the poetic engine and form varies—from prose poems and free verse to villanelles, even a pantoum—these poems, like the orb they celebrate, also honor cosmic order and the need for order in the restless human mind.

>   —Catharine Savage Brosman, poet and critic, Professor Emerita of French, Tulane University, recent works: *Southwestern Women Writers and the Vision of Goodness* (2016), and *A Memory of Manaus: Poems* (2017)

The Night's Magician is a fascinating collection of poems that sparkle with imagination and shared love for the orb we all know and love. These poets raise the bar as they focus on the moon with a shared reverence and awe. They make our hearts beat faster and truer with the beams of their poetry. Sue Walker and Philip Kolin have crafted a truly beautiful anthology in which poem after poem folds itself around the ever familiar, intimate presence of the moon.

> —William Ferris, author of *The South in Color: A Visual Journal.*

This brilliant collection is a demonstration of the universality of the poet's gaze at the moon. Along with the human heart, the moon is perhaps the most suited for consideration by the poet—a pool and a mirror, our closest yet unreachable neighbor. Sharing their visions with us the poets in *The Night's Magician* demonstrate the universality of the moon, our shared neighbor and mirror to us all.

> —Carlos Dews, Ph.D., M.F.A. writer and professor, Director, Institute for Creative Writing and Literary Translation at John Cabot University in Rome.

If you are old enough to remember 1953, Dean Martin crooning *When the moon hits your eye like a big pizza pie, that's amore,* you will fall in love all over again when your eyes feast on poems in *The Night's Magician.* Some poems explore the moon's relation to earth and create hymns to our life on this planet. Other lush poems look closely at the natural world and the moon's physical cycles to see how they each reflect an individual life. Several poets depict its gravitational pull that produces ocean tide, body tide and the slight lengthening of the day. Others delve into the moon's mysterious indifference, what it coolly withholds, a puzzle that can't be solved, that prompts dogs to bay their hearts out. All in all, *The Night's Magician* provides a torch that the heart can follow through the darkness.

> —Vivian Shipley poet and Distinguished Professor, Southern Connecticut State University, recent works: *Perennial* (Negative Capability, 2015) and *All of Your Messages Have Been Erased* (Louisiana Literature Press, 2010).

Everyone is a moon, and has a dark side which he never shows to anybody.
—Mark Twain, *Pudd'nhead Wilson*

The moon lives in the lining of your skin.
—Pablo Neruda

Fly me to the moon; let me play among the stars.
—Frank Sinatra

O, swear not by the moon, that inconstant moon/that monthly changes in her circled orb./Lest thy love prove likewise variable.
—Shakespeare, *Romeo and Juliet*

The moon for all her light and grace has never learned to know her place.
—Robert Frost

Follow your inner moonlight; don't hide the madman.
—Allen Ginsberg

If the moon smiles, she would resemble you. You leave the same impression of something beautiful, but annihilating.
—Sylvia Plath, "The Rival"

It is a most beautiful and delightful sight to behold the body of the moon.
—Galileo

And the sun will be turned into darkness and the moon into blood, before the great and glorious day of the Lord shall come.
—Acts 2:20

Years ago the moon was an inspiration to poets and an opportunity for lovers. Ten years from now it will be just another airport.
—Emmanuel G. Mesthene, *Technology and Change: Its Implications for Man and Society*, 1977

There are nights when the wolves are silent and only the moon howls.
—George Carlin

The sun is down and the moon is pretty–it's time to ramble.
—Elvis Presley

The future is like the daytime moon, a diffident but faithful companion, so elegant as to be almost invisible, an inconspicuous marvel.
—Robert Grudin

the NIGHT'S MAGICIAN
Poems about the Moon

Edited by
PHILIP C. KOLIN AND SUE BRANNAN WALKER

Negative Capability PRESS

The Night's Magician: Poems about the Moon

© September 2018, Negative Capability Press
All rights reserved.
Edited by Philip C. Kolin and Sue Brannan Walker

Cover and Interior Design by Megan Cary

ISBN 978-0-9986777-4-3
Library of Congress Control Number: 2018950986

Negative Capability Press
64 Ridgelawn Drive East
Mobile, Alabama 36608
(251) 591-2922

www.negativecapabilitypress.org
facebook.com/negativecapabilitypress

PREFACE

This anthology of nearly 80 new and original poems about the moon was occasioned by three spectacular lunar events in 2017. The first occurred on February 10th when a "snow moon" was covered by the earth's shadow in what astronomers have labeled a "penumbral/lunar eclipse." The second and third more dramatic events both happened in August. A partial eclipse was visible across five continents on August 7th and 8th. Adding to these spectacular celestial phenomena was the "Great Solar Eclipse" witnessed across a wide swath of the United States. Playing hide and seek, the moon in 2017 was indeed the subject of much amazement, study, mediation, and predictions. Rarely could one generation have observed so many heavenly events in a year.

While these recent cosmic phenomena initially inspired *The Night's Magician*, our motivation goes much deeper; in fact, our rationale can be seen as historical as well as metaphysical. From the earliest written records, e.g., *The Sumerian Temple Hymns* or *Genesis*, the moon has aroused a galaxy of emotions: fascination and fear; calm and calamity; beauty and upheaval; flux and eternal sameness. Full moons, for instance, have received numerous and often contradictory interpretations. They can predict when delivery rooms will overflow and also when aberrant behavior will be at its zaniest. As the earth's closest neighbor, the moon has also inspired much research and attention from numerous disciplines ranging from selenography to astronomy and meteorology and from art to mythography, not to mention an abundance of science fiction films and novels. As the subject of scientific investigations, the moon, too, has shed light on ecology, the trajectory of planets and comets, and on the future of space exploration.

Theologically, the moon with its lunar calendar as opposed to a sidereal one has been the timekeeper for sacred events including Passover, Easter, and Ramadan. Following a lunar calendar, the Chinese Mid-Autumn Festival is a jubilant national holiday celebrating and even worshipping the moon when people eat mooncakes, drink osmanthus wine, and hang red lanterns up and down the streets. Many of the poems in *The Night's Magician* capture the ways in which various cultures speak about things lunar.

Over the millennia it has been poets and musicians who have exhibited a special affinity to the moon and its various phases and paradoxical manifestations. Rejuvenated or dismayed by its luminescence, some famous musical compositions include Beethoven's *Moonlight Sonata*, Debussy's *Clair de Lune*, and Schubert's *Rosamunde*. In poetry, the moon is a symbol of love, too, the simulacrum of desire in its fulfillment of a long-awaited climax. Reflecting its paradoxical glow, though, the moon can also symbolize an "inconstant" sphere "that monthly changes in her circled orb" (*Romeo and Juliet*), and thus bodes ill for lovers seeking fulfillment. The moon has also been invoked as the dividing line between heavenly and earthly love. As John Donne professed in his iconic poem "A Valediction: Forbidding Mourning," "Dull sublunary lovers" are destined for disappointment; they grow pale and fade away like the descending moon itself. But those lovers like the poet John Donne and his wife who strive for a spiritual consummation reach the apogee of desire. Readers will find that the poems in *The Night's Magician* offer plentiful takes on both sublunary and spiritual lovers and events.

Like the wandering moon, the poems in this collection reflect its many phases, and the diverse styles, genres, and themes that represent them. The shortest poem here is only six lines long (suggesting the silvered, crescent moon) while the longest beams over two pages (symbolizing a full moon). Yet both poems say something essential about the moon and the speakers' relationship to it. Some of the poems here follow formal poetic conventions, echoing the trumpeting phrasings of a Shakespeare or an Alexander Pope while others are closer to the iconoclastic works of the New York School of Poetry. In fact, several poems in *The Night's Magician* experiment boldly with conventions of space, speaker, images and orchestrated interruptions. Expressing the variety of responses to the moon, this anthology features lyrical as well as satirical poems and sacramental ones, too. Some of the poems here in fact might be read as meditations about the moon's ineluctable place in God's gaze. Though Scripture terms the moon the "lesser light to rule the night," (*Genesis* 1:16) that designation has not diminished its poetic influence.

We are honored to include work here by a host of distinguished poets. One is a former U.S. Poet Laureate, many are state laureates, and several are founders and/or editors of major journals. Contributors have also won impressive honors ranging from an American Book Award to a Pushcart Prize to a Robert Frost Medal to the Thomas Merton Prize in Poetry of the Sacred. Others have received fellowships including a Guggenheim and a PEN American Literary Award as well as residencies at influential art and writers' colonies. But whether established or emerging voices, all the poets in *The Night's Magician* have written eloquently and innovatively about a skyload of moons, luminous or beclouded, new or old, full or crescent, and have even ventured into the dark side of the moon.

We are indebted to these poets who have made this anthology possible and our work as editors a joy. We are also grateful to Megan Cary who designed the cover art and interior and enhanced this collection befitting that magnificent magician of the night, the ever-wandering moon.

– Philip C. Kolin and Sue Brannan Walker
September 2018

TABLE OF CONTENTS

A

Ralph Adamo	1
Alice J. Aldridge	3
Maureen Alsop	4

B

Ned Balbo	5
Mary Jo Bang	7
Frederick W. Bassett	8
Michael Bassett	10
Joseph Bathanti	12
Jill Peláez Baumgaertner	14
Jack B. Bedell	15
Stephen Behrendt	16
Kris Bigalk	17
John Bradley	19
Kim Bridgford	20
John J. Brugaletta	21

C

Peter Neil Carroll	22
Kelly Cherry	23
Michael Chitwood	24

D

Jeremy DeFatta	25
Will Dowd	26
Mircea Dan Duta	27
Stuart Dybek	28

E

Martin Espada	30

F

Malaika Favorite	31
Gary Fincke	33
Deborah Ford	34
Chris Forhan	35

G

Maria Mazziotti Gillan	36
Vicki Graham	38
Willliam Greenway	39

H

Twyla M. Hansen	41
James Harms	43
Dixon Hearne	44

Kathleen Hellen 45

Lou Ella Hickman, I.W.B.S. 46

J

Angela Jackson-Brown 47

K

Tim Kahl 48

George Kalamaras 49

David Kirby 51

Brian Jerrold Koester 52

Philip C. Kolin 53

Ted Kooser 55

L

Bill Lavender 56

Sydney Lea 57

Philip L. Levin 58

Michael A. Lofaro 59

M

Peter Makuck 60

Paul Mariani 61

Tod Marshall 63

Karen McPherson	64
Peter Meinke	65
Caryn Mirriam-Goldberg	66
Robert Morgan	67
Mary Murphy	68

N

Robert Nazarene	70
Nick Norwood	71

P

Linda Pastan	72
Joseph Pearce	73
Marge Piercy	74

R

Kevin Rabas	75
Doug Ramspeck	76
Diane Raptosh	77
Joseph Ross	78
Jason Roush	80

S

Sonia Sanchez	81
Pat Schneider	85
Martha Serpas	87
Marley Stuart	88
Virgil Suárez	89
Mary Swander	90

T

Leonard A. Temme	93
James Torrens, S.J.	94
Jacqueline Allen Trimble	95

W

Sue Brannan Walker	96
Shanti Weiland	98
Carey Scott Wilkerson	100

Z

Jianqing Zheng	101
Contributors' Notes	103

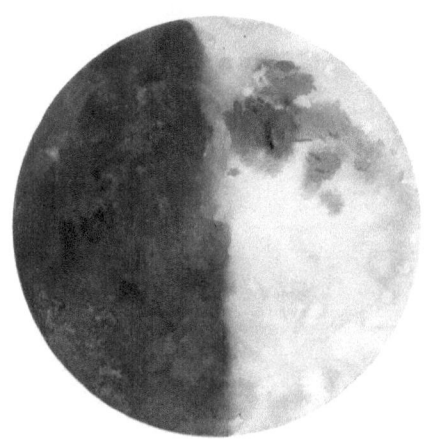

There You Are
RALPH ADAMO

Sometimes I try to read the moon like a book
as if it were an old tree full of stories
stuck in the asphalt night
I laugh along with the moon at the names
we give it, the measures we take from its stoic
punctual self, the idea that an idea
born on earth could be of the slightest
moment to this big rock caught
in the net of our girth

For years, I tried to see the moon
through tree limbs—red bud, sycamore,
oak of course, pine, so many, all to catch
a glimpse of her complicity.
I was not convinced the moon wasn't
hearing it all—the songs chiefly,
wafting away from the mouth of pain (or
joy—mustn't deny it) toward trembling
ears, among them hers, the sly moon, the
uninvited one, clothed in cold light, her
pitted face half guarded by a silver scarf —

The moon has taken nothing away
Nothing from anyone
Let others make of the moon what they
will, legend or warning, arbiter of the wave
and the madness beneath
The moon's indifference is the key
The rest of us howl and dance

Here's a question: is the moon
sending secret messages to select dead
ones? There in the moist earth —fragments

of themselves — are they receiving
orders that read as music?

If the phases of that old woman, that cold
stone, that pocked mirror, that hanging
basket of shadows is connoting
anything, I do not believe it is the
unpardonable mystery you wish
to unbury…nor a chart
detailing the births of the fastest horses…
and not even a crooked glass corner down
the street from where you are going to die.
Let's call the phases she wheezes through
by the names of famous clowns, or
discontinued brands of smoke. That much
we can account for, trying to sleep.

On his way off the planet my friend said,
'Keep your eye on the moon, your poetry'

He was not an ancient poet of ancient
China, but a river seer, a physician of the
line between word and speech, between
sound and song, between sadness and
death. Steeled connoisseur of the ineffable –
dressed as a young man in a hurry. My
friend knew the moon as an equal. His
words made the moon pause and cast
a glance in my trembling direction. Oh.
There you are.
Said the clowning moon. Said the somber
stone. Said the brightness so softly
enfolding the time of my life on earth.

Moon Delights
ALICE J. ALDRIDGE

The moon was a dinner guest at our house peeking through Mama's polka dot curtains. We feasted on moonbeams, Barq's *Moon-Glo*, and my favorite, moon pies, all that white marshmallow sent down from the moon's face itself. Papa never failed to have some of his favorite moon juice on the sly, that homemade moonshine. We joked and said that Papa was eclipsed, but he said he was just a little lightheaded. We celebrated special dining events every time there was a month with a blue moon in it. That's when mother brought out her wedding china—her Harvest Moon plates, saucers, and cups. Till this day I can still hear the Marcels crooning "Blue Moon," and each one hungering for a Blue Moon Pie. Unfortunately, I could not find one at Mooney's Supermarket. When Bobby Joe came courting my younger sister, Luna Lynn, he wore Rick Owens' Moon Boots which cast a swathe of moonlight through our door. I recall that my sister put on a false jewel tiara that looked like a crescent moon; she never glowed brighter. My recommendation to young ladies looking to get married is to find a man with a moon face, someone who will plant moon vines in your garden and store plenty of moon pies in the pantry. Maybe he will take you on a honeymoon to the Sea of Tranquility.

Selenomancy
MAUREEN ALSOP

In the year of ghost-holly-noon in winter and chestnut sky at night—the dead's voices carry dowry-bells and silver spools along the river's collarbone.

So emerald the quiet. Only shadow in green undertow.

A stone glows a black fire in the small woods, her mouth— drags so slow—the language entering a terrain divided by sun: a valley of tree-casts, check points.

When she stumbled he wiped the taste of moth from her lip. The creek curdled in the heat.

Already masses of lily shift the breeze. She fades halfway above   and begins.

Moonglow[1]
(For my adoptive mother Betty, and for Jane)

NED BALBO

Outside at dusk, watching the full moon inch

beyond the treetops in a sky still blue,
I find myself appreciating speed,
    time's tidal passage leading back,
each new phase surfacing, a sky still black
      beyond the blue, and you
        singing the tune "Moonglow"
      in our split-level ranch,
your voice and gentle strum produced by memory's need.

You learned guitar so I could learn guitar
then gave up lessons I kept practicing.
(The full moon in its rising doesn't stop
    or alter its ascent or course
whether or not the night sky fills with stars.)
      You sang with so much feeling
        (twilight: a moment passing
      from verse to final measure),
but moonrise only goes in one direction—up—

and memory only backward, further still....
Above the treetops where the clouds are shards
the moon rekindles temporarily,
    who's watching? In the fretwork of
its climb, an inlaid dot appears to move—
      From you I learned the chords,
        the melody and words,
      the lift and minor fall...
My wife beside me, head bowed, reads on quietly—

---

[1]   "Moonglow," music by Will Hudson and Irving Mills, lyrics by Eddie DeLange, 1933.

Sometimes I think about your hands, your past,
arthritic branches, weightless in the way,
left to the tangled dark...The moon has risen,
    carrying its cobalt glow
and moonstruck lyrics, downward stroke, the slow
       progression of a day
        like others, unlike any—
       The book is closed at last,
a new page marked: *Tomorrow*. What else are we given?

The sky, the wind, the darkness over all—

A satellite and stars to light the world.
The dark trees' denizens, the smell (metallic)
of wet soil, quiet hours.
The unknown, absent lives of passing strangers
      that disappear, withheld;
      the known lives that unfold
      in moon-glow, visible—
A loved one close at hand, the memory of music.

Children Were Erasing Their Faces
MARY JO BANG

Children were erasing their faces. So it seemed. Let me know, he said, if I begin to play the part of a metronome. The glass a stem in his hand. The girl staring at the glazed school window. It closed, opened, closed, an overactive hand. How many times? The road in the Ozarks flooded one summer but machismo told the father he needed to take a risk. He listened and did it. Time buried him in cinders. Was one allowed to comment on the fact that an artificial heart has something metronomic about it. That unending lub-lub-dub. The shortened sense of time at a window. She was surprised by the way the moon drifted in, noticing only after the fact she wasn't in the same place. A tractor skirted a green rectangle. An empire of trouble remained stuffed inside a blue bottle that matched the embers of St. Elmo's fire. A paper pistol went off in May and the race across a lake began. That's how she remembered it. That was not, however, how it happened. Instead, she stood at a rail and watched waves sent back by a cat slapping the dock. A lightning strike revealed the predicament of a body refusing to give in. The moon was inattentive.

The Moon as Witness
FREDERICK W. BASSETT

The low tide pulls me from our house
near the beach into a moonless
hour of the night.
The stars bathe the breaking waves
with a delicate silver light,
as I follow the water's edge
to my favorite dunes.

Reclining in wind-sculpted sand,
sea oats dancing above me,
I watch the moon rise
above the ocean at its own pace,
its beams shimmering a wake
straight into my eyes
as if I mattered in the scheme of things.

Thus, ennobled by the moon,
I transcend the gravity
of the day to hunt with Orion
near the edge of the Milky Way
where the rivers run crystal clear
and the forests never hear
the echoing sound of an ax.

From the dark woods behind me,
the hoots of a barred owl
pull me back into the dunes that buffer
Hilton Head Island's last strip
of wild oceanfront that, all too soon,
will be consumed by condos.

The owl repeats its warning,
a prophet crying in the wilderness.
The moon's wake trembles
across the choppy sea
as it follows me up the beach
until I take the path home.

Returning and Returning
MICHAEL BASSETT

All my life's a circle, sunrise and sundown
The moon rolls through the nighttime, till the daybreak comes around
The reappearance of the light is the same as the survival of the soul.

    —Victor Hugo

I.

In the late-night café, a man screams at his friend,
"Most problems can't be fixed by legislation.
Hell, most problems can't be fixed!"
What the moon hears is "My hope has become like the coffee in this mug,
a small tight ring."

A girl studies the windowsill
where she's collected empty cocoons.
She prays for what she may become
when her shell falls away.
What the moon hears is
"White candle, love water, flow into my body.
Energize every cell."

II.

We are a legacy of landings and striving.
We are craters of possibility. Always
rising behind us is the memory of our earlier selves. Always
inside us like rings in tree trunks, records of our longings,
promises of so many risings.

Night after night, the moon recycles it imperatives:
Rewrite The Bill of Dreams
in the left ventricle of humanity's heart.
Spell all the words with vowels of travel, zest, and mystery.
Refuse all that does not enrich and quicken the blood.
Reject all metaphors but those of return.
Return to the open heart and the helping hand.
Return to earnest messy complicated but unsophisticated
love of the world.

Return to big stories, songs crackling with sparks
daring conflagration of nerve.

III.

Oh, silver confetti drizzler,
fling your snowflake, soapflake, ash flake dye.
Bone bleach, sea swell, rise.

Oh, hot candy apple,
thumb smudge on the face of wonder,
poetry-pockmarked dandy, return and renew.

Oh, sailing ocher kite on the brink of night,
yellow jacket queen on the front porch of our dreams,
gunner's, lover's, harvest moon,
jazzy June, va va voom,
Intercede. Translate. Transform.

Anson Moon
JOSEPH BATHANTI

I will incline my ear to a parable.
                              Psalm 48:5

Should we not find the way
and darkness claim much more,

Jacob and I'll remain
cold without fire or light –

pockets empty, no coat,
cow-bellow off sounding –

in Anson woods tonight.
Worn and thorn-whipped, my son

reckons our plight, and clings
to me. I sight the trees

to beckon the way out;
but, dark, the sky confounds.

Lost he'll not utter, though
at seven his penchant

for Heaven claims its cost
is wandering, and not

believing, too far. Yet
he prays, he confesses,

to God. The way, of course,
though hidden, in ruins,

is with us – here. We must
simply ask and listen

for the current swaddling
the Pee Dee, cottonmouths

cuddling white Sycamore
roots, squawking Mergansers,

Kingfishers blue, roosting
the night, George Washington

Little's line shack listing
in the logging road. *There*:

crowning red oaks seeded
two hundred years ago

by Lord Anson, sprawling
Fred Poisson's pond, it gleams –

the snow moon, scrawling shore
and swale alabaster,

so loomed, recalled and near,
we step through it and fall

asleep in the clearing
of prayer's hypnotic thrall.

Real Presence, Moon
JILL PELÁEZ BAUMGAERTNER

Silk saucer,
Runnels and lilt,
Lyric devoid of breath,
Fickle yet faithful costumer,
You are massive at the horizon,
A silver sliver as you wane.
Mostly at night but some
Times, you changeable
Waif, there you are at
Morning rise.

I know only this, silent coin:
You hide then appear
At cloud's convenience.
Little white rabbit soft
In your light, or stately
Monstrance, blank wafer,
I ask you:
Are you blood
Or mere harbinger?

Course Correction
JACK B. BEDELL

After the river showed up in the front yard
        everything in the house began to lean.

The water drew us to the front porch
        when it was low on its banks, pushed us

toward the back walls whenever it rose
        at night. The first full moon yanked us

toward the windowsill so fierce
        we had to spin the foot of our bed

around to face the lapping waves.
        Daylight helped keep things settled

enough for work to get done. Old growth
        timber still had to be planed for lumber,

upland traps collected for winter food.
        Even then, the river's flow conversed

in ways the woods never could,
        and the world would not untilt itself,

whether the moon waned new, or no.

Annie and the Sturgeon Moon
STEPHEN BEHRENDT

This is the moon that has befriended her,
unlike its eleven rude brothers
who peer in her windows, follow her,
startle her while she bathes, unabashed,
innocent breeze thin through her slotted window.
But the sturgeon moon, ruddy with the latent heat
that pools at night in the low spots,
hangs over the tamarack bogs redolent with tannin:
he keeps her soundless company in the August silence
broken only by the owls' cries, the pulsing
of the great white stallion's hoofbeats
racing his demons down the east-lying pasture
beneath its white benevolent beams.
The old Menomini woman who lived on this land
a century and a half ago, who visits her some nights,
the cool whiteness lighting her deep-lined oval face,
told her the moons' names, described their varied faces
rising big and pumpkin-hued over Stevens Ridge.
The sturgeon moon loved her people,
blessed their fishing on the swift brown river
where they hauled out the log-like sturgeon
under his ancient deep approving gaze,
his broad smile flashing silver sparks
off their glistening lumpy leathern lengths.
This moon tells her secrets, long-forgotten tales
of those whose land this was before, under other night skies,
like the old woman whose moon-white face
none sees but her — and the great white stallion
whose apples Annie places on the fenceposts,
unafraid despite the looming woods' immensity
because her sturgeon moon has her hand fast.

Moonstruck
KRIS BIGALK

His deep, honeyed,
almost-
prayers echoed
in my ears on
good mornings, his voice
and the newborn
summer filled my
eyes, flooded
my ears like
sunlight.

His words lassoed
the edges of the June
moon, his silver kisses
tasted of salt
and beer as we
rocked, his boat a cradle
underneath the canopy of pines.

Now all of that
a whisper
evaporating into chilly
silent evenings spent
in different time zones,
and when he's
lonely, the harvest
moon rising
over the lake, he
doesn't call, doesn't
speak, just
a photo of the scarlet

moon, *wish you
were here*
texted in the voice
of the man
who used
to tell me I
was beautiful.

Twenty Questions for the Moon
JOHN BRADLEY

How is it I can fit the Nile River in an eyedropper
but not your delicious light? Spilling, plunging,
surging—which best describes the hunger of your
Sea of Fecundity? If I make a crooked circle
with forefinger and thumb, hold it up until it
surrounds you, will you blind me, or make me
surrender to wakeful sleep? On that plaza in Manaus
named for you? What was it Li Po said
when he sank into your long cadaverous arms?
Tell us, why is NASA hiding our kidnapped children
in colonies on Mars? Plunging, surging, spilling—
which best describes your vaporous white hair?
On that steep street in Galway named for you?
When Galileo gazed through his telescope
at your granulated flesh, how softly did he say,
I am made of moon and web and ravenous crumb?
Do you prefer being compared to a peeled lemon,
slice of unripe banana, or hammered tin head?
On that back street in Reykjavik named for you?
Is it true you keep a list of every fool
who ever mooned you? Surging, spilling, plunging—
how is it you shadow me by day, I shadow you
by night? O carnivorous moon, may I serve you
at the Banquet of Luminous Beings? On plates
of damp moonstone? With narcotic blooms
of moonflower? In Novosibirsk, near
the unfinished nuclear waste repository,
in the middle of the roundabout named for you?
What was it you told Li Po when he embraced
your surging, spilling, plunging arms? When
will we build a delirious wall to keep you
from seeping into our dream reservoir? Why
did you tell those moonstruck kids NASA kidnapped
and sent to Mars, *If you wear silver gloves
no one will be able to withstand
the beauty of your vaporous hands*?

Something Happened
KIM BRIDGFORD

Something happened to the moon: it fell.
It was not the smiling moon I grew up with;
It tasted daily life and found it cruel.

Such happy characters were once in style,
The dish and spoon and I all friends. Then life.
Something happened to the moon. It fell,

And with it came hypocrisy and guile.
The upward look became a downward laugh.
Tasting daily life to find it cruel,

Substituting heaven-sight for gruel,
I felt, somehow, that I was not enough.
Something happened to the moon. I fell,

And, on the way, I felt less admirable.
I drew my cynicism from its sheath,
For I tasted daily life and found it cruel.

I was born, I walked the earth, and that was all.
The moon was bud, and flower, and lost leaf.
Something happened. The moon and I both fell.
We tasted daily life and found it cruel.

The Moon, That Seeming Disk
JOHN J. BRUGALETTA

I thought I saw the man-in-the-moon once,
a feeble figure even then—but never again.
Likewise with the constellations. Oh the big dipper
was okay, but as for the rest, it was tumult.
Either I'm not perceptive enough, or else
the ancients didn't have enough to do.

And now that I think about it, the stars only
look close to one another, as if they were pinpricks
in a one-layer tin sky. And the moon, ah yes
the moon, that seeming disk of polished silver,
was ripped by caesarian from the earth's belly
by some wandering asteroid and flung into orbit
around its mother like a child hanging desperately
to her apron strings of gravity.

                                        And yet its own
gravity hauls into motion the tides, without which
our ancestors would never have scuttled onto land,
changing fins into legs, lungs taking charges of air,
standing at last upright, brain in its ivory box,
rounded while contorted, billions of neurons
that somehow became aware of themselves.

And then there are those lovers reproducing
after gazing at that tranquil face, that lovely orb.

Moon Lit
PETER NEIL CARROLL

Tule fog obscures the sky, a wraith
across the early night, the trick's
to drive behind a pair of crimson lights,
not too close to chance a sudden fright,
not too far to lose their bright
until a shift of height dispels the mist
and lunar clarity exalts the sight,
silhouettes trees, a house, a kitchen
lit, the pavement white, the midnight
glows, the blackness shines.

Full Moon
KELLY CHERRY

Last night, a full moon, small and bald as a baby
and caught in a crib of tangled winter branches:
Rock-a-bye, I thought, *rock-a-bye, baby.*

I'm getting old and foolish, yet the moon's
hypnotic light, dangling from the night sky,
impressed upon my simple heart a truth

so very true that I had overlooked it:
survival is not resurrection but
renewal—renewal of seasons, generations,

our feelings, even. Lives wear out and drop
away and we must grieve until ourselves,
too, have fallen, bitten apples on the ground.

How splendid, then, the newborn child, the young
Whose lively song has still to be sung.

Quiet and Quieter Still
MICHAEL CHITWOOD

The hunter's moon brings the King Tide,
gargling up into the storm drains,
seeping over the sea walls, salting
the not-so-fresh fresh water.
The moon makes its own path on the water
for the hunter king to walk.
Stealth is his stock in trade,
no fanfare, no brocade, no trumpet blare.
He will have what he will have
with the patience of the snare.

All Roads Lead to the Moon
JEREMY DeFATTA

Whether a point of navigation,
or a source of light far from home,
the moon is icon and
sacred candelabrum to explorers.

For a few short loops about the sun
human, mortal man set vacuum-sealed foot
upon the moon's silvery dust slopes,
some very nearly leaping from there
to the stars themselves.

The names of heroes, idols, demigods—
Armstrong, Aldrin, Collins—lit the fires
of wanderlust, the need to discover and
experience something truly alien, for
so few others. And then the fires ceased.

But must it always be so? Is it too
late to become explorers once more?
We are content to sit in Cheeto-dust
and breathe in xenophobia-scented candles,
picking fun at pictures of crying celebrities
eating sandwiches on park benches.

Are we of the same blood as those classical heroes?
Can we possibly be worthy again to once more
tread the black between us and our closest
astronomical neighbor, and in so doing
make for ourselves a newer,
better, smarter home?

A Little Procedural Candor
WILL DOWD

Any poet should be able to write a poem about the moon.
A hundred of them. Hung upside down. Hungover.
The Hunger Moon. It's low-hanging fruit. Babies
reach for it. So what's my problem? What's my hang-up?
When Jean-Paul Sartre told his grandfather
he wanted to become a poet, the old man scoffed,
*A poet is someone who promises to show you the moon
and ends up showing you his derrière.* It's possible
I made that story up. Just now. On the spot.
The truth is I used to go there when I was a kid.
Most float up to the corner of a ceiling. Become
a fly. A cobweb. But I was an overachiever.
An overshooter. Some of the craters were small
and some were big. The dust was like flour. It clung.
It smelled like spent gunpowder. I never went
to the dark side so don't ask. I drew a map once
but it was a child's map. I never told anyone.
Dogs followed me. Howling. It's funny. You
become a poet, despite poverty, despite obscurity,
because you sense, in the anachronism of measured lines,
a way to explain how it feels to exist in two places
simultaneously. Then, after years of study, after years
of instruction, you settle for describing the common
housefly in such painstaking detail that the reader,
in a moment of unthinking irritation, swats the page.

Periphery
MIRCEA DAN DUTA

The Moon is a larger village,
where everybody knows everybody,
everything is close to all
and nothing is too different of anything,
the light of the sun is neighboring
the dark side of the place,
Armstrong Valley continues
Mount Gagarin
and I go skiing on both of them
together with the selfie of my ghost.
They call this
a suburban inferiority complex.
They talk like this also about
Bratislava, Prague, Vienna,
the Earth itself, Venus and Pluto.
But it is only on the Earth
that they are afraid
the Moon could fall on them.

Phases
STUART DYBEK

The darkness felt disorienting, more sweltering than the sunbeaten day, tacky against your skin like the tar roof under bare feet. When I heard my mother say the moon was going through faces I wondered if she meant it was making faces at us. The yellow housedress she was wearing for a nightgown was stuck to her by sweat. She still wore her glasses as if she might be going to sleep with them on. Below, our neighborhood was sketched in electricity, but she stood staring up at the unplugged moon as if it really was making faces. I thought of her dreamily staring at her own face in her bureau mirror on nights when before going to sleep she'd give her hair a hundred strokes. The bureau's drawers were stuffed with faces, shoeboxes of photos, the hundreds of snapshots she had taken with her Brownie. My mother loved taking pictures. Without seeming to intrude, it made her part of the action: weddings in the small polka halls of corner bars, first Communions, her brothers back from war and still in uniform, people in our neighborhood like the blind newspaperman and his burning ashcan, or Enrique, the tamale man who sold from a cart that wore a sombrero tamales his wife made, girls playing hopscotch, her lady friends over for coffee and Tupperware, drenched guys giving rides on their Harleys through the spray of jacked-open hydrants, all there in the bureau drawers. The killer heat wave seemed to have bent the laws we'd lived by, including the rules for going to sleep. It felt as if, without having to say so, people in our neighborhood—maybe the whole city—had agreed that it was necessary to allow for hydrant-flooded streets, for drinking beer from tubs of ice on the front steps, for being in general a little more crazy than usual. People talked more and when they did they told more stories. Maybe the heat had bent the very sound of words. When I heard my mother say *going through faces*, I could imagine the moon's face magnified in her bureau mirror, silver makeup pitted with acne. Or a haloed holy face stamped on a medal. Or a mug shot moon tarnished with stubble, keeping company with the nocturnal Most Wanted faces of murderers and kidnappers. We were three stories closer to the moon than usual. My father had hauled a couple mattresses up the fire escape and onto the flat roof because, despite the rickety whirring window fans, our flat was suffocating. Back then, the only places in our neighborhood with air-conditioning were the Marshal Square Theater and the Cermak Bowl.

"We'll sleep like sailors under that stars," my father said.

Not that there were stars in a city firmament that smog and mercury vapor streetlights had permanently colored an opaque maroon.

"We'll sleep under the moon," mom said, "They say the moon gives you special dreams."

"They who? I never heard that," my father said.

"It's a well known fact," mom said, "Try to remember them so we can all compare moon dreams when we wake in the morning."

"What if I don't have dreams," I asked.

"Don't worry, sweetie," she said, "of course you will. The moon has its phases and so does everything. So do we. Sleeping, dreaming, waking up to a new day.

A baldy bean whose head you'd rub for luck if you could reach it.

A face with smeared mascara.

A locket that opens on a blurred, ancient face looking out from behind a cracked crystal.

A moon that lowers its visor tonight and turns inward.

Sleeping. Thunder. Waking up. Sleeping. Summer rain.

Basswoods along the curb dripping into reflected sky.

Asking Questions of the Moon
MARTIN ESPADA

*Some blind girls
ask questions of the moon
and spirals of weeping
rise through the air.*
       —Federico Garcia Lorca

As a boy, I stood guard in right field, lazily punching my glove,
keeping watch over the ballgame and the moon as it rose
from the infield, asking questions of the moon about the girl
with long blonde hair in the back of my classroom, who sat with me
when no one else would, who talked to me when no one else would,
who laughed at my jokes when no one else would, until the day
her friend sat beside us and whispered to her behind that long hair,
and the girl asked me, as softly as she could: *Are you a spic?*
And I, with a swarm of words in my head, could only think to say:
Yes, I am. She never spoke to me again, and as I thought of her
in the outfield the moon fell from the sky, tore through the webbing
of my glove, and smacked me in the eye. Blinded, I wept, kicked
the moon at my feet, and loudly blamed the webbing of my glove.

A Naked Poem
MALAIKA FAVORITE

I am sitting on the shore
Lying to the river
Reciting all the reasons I can't jump in

For five minutes
I held out my pen
And pierced the moon

There it was dangling on the tip,
Daring me to become liquid
The river wants to suck my toes

A man I knew
Once told me it was a sensual experience
Far better than natural sex

I resented his tongue
Imagining all the toes he had sucked
But the river had my attention

The mud oozing between my fingers
And the driftwood, hard
Anchoring my back

The moon left me for an oak tree
And danced with it as I swayed
To her lulling song

When the dance became steamy
A cloud covered their nakedness
Humming: silence is the best music

Then there was rain
Raw drops pouring into the river
And over me

The more the rain wet me
The more liquid I became
So wet I had to peel off

All that separated
Me from the mouth of the river
I bathed in the light of moon

Blue Moon
GARY FINCKE

In 1977, just after my vasectomy,
a man in Somalia contracted
the last natural case of smallpox.
Forty years now, as long ago
as the death of Elvis, but there are
17 million vaccine doses in storage,
"Just in case," according to
the Elvis sighters of disease.
Though why not, those germs sampled
and stored as well, a neighbor,
each August, playing "Blue Moon" at sunset,
spinning it 42 times to honor
the Elvis life span. I've thanked him
for not adding the posthumous years,
for not playing the all-day Elvis canon,
those songs so common I anticipate
the words. In Bangladesh, the word
for smallpox is the same as the word
for springtime, another version
of common, but I ask my neighbor
why not "Blue Moon of Kentucky" or
"When my Blue Moon Turns to Gold Again,"
and he asks, "What were you doing when
Elvis died?" and I know I was listening
to the cries of my last-born son, that
my wife was feeding him, give or take
an hour, and I was wishing him
the good luck of the gold moon because
chance had already been recorded.

Sitting Alone with the Moon
DEBORAH FORD

On the Great Plains of North Dakota at night,
You can read the poems of Li Bo
Without the aid of artificial light.

Think of the galaxies, the moon so white;
The midnight sky is all aglow
On the Great Plains of North Dakota at night.

China's T'ang poet provides some insight
When you're sitting alone near a sunflower meadow
Without the aid of artificial light.

The pounding wind exerts its might
Stalks and grasses whipping to and fro
On the Great Plains of North Dakota at night.

Stifle the impulse to recite
A line or two. Just sip the Bordeaux
Without the aid of artificial light.

It's the hunter's moon. Sit tight.
Look for it on the far side of Fargo.
On the Great Plains of North Dakota at night
Enjoy the heavens without the aid of artificial light.

Luna ex Machina
CHRIS FORHAN

Like a knucklebone: stuck, freakish and blue
in the black—this late, that's how it occurs to us.

Stabbed with a flagpole, it's dead.

Yet we pause in the parking lot, fumbling for keys, and glance
straight up into the weird heart of it.

Through the Buick's back window, between trees, it trails us.

Its low vowel yearns in Sinatra's throat.

But its thoughts keep to themselves, entering
the song only when the song goes silent.

Contemplating the Moon in My Seventy-Seventh Year
MARIA MAZZIOTTI GILLAN

As a girl, I was fascinated by the moon,
thought it was amazing in the dark Paterson sky.
I wrote hundreds of haiku about it.
I always saw it as some reflection of my longing
to live in a place far removed from my ordinary life.

In 1969, in married student housing at Rutgers,
I watched with my two young children,
as Neil Armstrong on the Apollo 11 mission
walked on the moon. It seemed
unbelievable that these figures could be walking
on that cratered surface.

Today, more than fifty years later, I read
that the moon is drifting away from the earth.
Did you know the dark side of the moon is a myth?

Now, the moon, has become a symbol for what is left
of my life, all those craters that trip us up so often,
so we're unable to walk without falling,
like the other day, when I waited for almost an hour
for someone to pick me up off the porch where I had fallen.

I must accept that the landscape of old age is like the surface
of the moon. It has so many places to fall.
As a girl, I made up stories about its cratered surface,
the faces I imagined lived in it.
I watched those astronauts on the moon, weightless in their space suits.
What did I know? I thought life would be easy,
and I would walk across it sure and strong;
instead now this shuffling gait.
I'd like to be weightless
like the men in their space suits.

No more broken bones.
No more pitfalls. No more grief.

Moon, each day, you wear a different face.
I still imagine you speak to me.
And you do, but the words I hear
cannot save me; it is your beauty,
as you skim across the night sky,
that lifts me up.

Waning
(For Nat, Lost to Alzheimer's)

VICKI GRAHAM

The moon a stone
and night a river washing
over it, grain by grain,
sanding it thin.

A new silence between us,
like the hush in the willows
after the thrush calls.
The notes still burn,
too sweet to swallow.

When you lost my name
I wondered: what will you say
when you lose my face?

Will your hands still remember mine?

The moon's waning crescent
hooks my heart. I lie awake
listening to you breathe 'til dawn.

Morning brings the silence of stones.
Not the silence of solace,
but the silence of sorrow at rest.

The moon a blade. Fog frayed silk.
Only a broken heart can sing
like the thrush, two notes at once,
duetting with itself.

Mississippi Moon
WILLIAM GREENWAY

Driving home from her father's house
back when we lived down here,
we'd turn the car lights off
and let the full moon silver
the road home. Sometimes we'd even
park and neck.

Back for a visit ten years along,
the skies busy approaching the millennium,
we go out into the evening to see
the eclipse like a plum with a cap
of sugar, Hale-Bopp chasing
its tail in the solar wind of the southwest,
Orion stalking the skies,
and Mars looking embarrassed
at the jewelry of Venus.

Portents all, prodigies, chimneys tumbling,
and horses eating each other in their stalls,
or at least beavers slapping the water in the dark,
and rippling, like a TV time warp, the stars
and ember eyes of frogs and gators lying on the lake.
Cottonmouths sleep on logs, their mouths
full of moonlight, tired as the snake that swallowed
its tail and made the world, and turtles—like
the one the Natives say the world rests on the back of—
poke their heads from the lake like toes.

No wonder people dream of abduction
by aliens on lonely back roads, city lights
so far way, these stars we thought we knew
moving farther from us and from each other.
So when a comet comes calling every
4,000 years or so, we go out and hold hands,

our faces upturned and white as two more moons,
Mars puts blusher over his cracks,
the moon veils her pitted face
and hides her belly with a dark muumuu,
Venus scintillates desperately,
and Orion loosens his belt and holds on,
none of us getting any younger.

Moonlight Meditations
TWYLA M. HANSEN

There was full magic streaming in the upstairs
farmhouse windows, enough to call us out
of sleep, stare at the odd silver light washing
over trees, henhouse, silo, clothesline, corncrib,
cattle, fences, hog shed, and ruts in the dirt lane.
Mother hushed us toward beds, but Father
opened his rough hands to ours, walked
us out into that grainy black-and-white film,
to gleams on the gravel, shimmers across
the stock tank, the skewed reflections on
broken windows of the old machine shed.
~
First it was that cow jumping over the moon,
Mother reading me a picture book, and Father
humming *By the Light of the Silvery Moon*.
Then Sinatra crooned *Fly Me to the Moon*,
which carried us to Beatles' *Mr. Moonlight*,
then Credence and *Bad Moon Rising*,
Stevens' *Moonshadow*, Morrison's *Moondance*,
on to Pink Floyd's *Dark Side of the Moon*:
hard as rock, the vocals, lyrics, guitar licks
that later flowed to our son and friends, teen
believers and full-blast from the basement.
~
The sun is male, we learn, the moon female—
his yang to her yin, together rotating in a black-
white circle, though nothing is straightforward
about ocean waves, wind, warmth, evaporation,
cloud, storm, lightning, thunder, fire, ashes, soil,
seeds, sprouts, sun, animals, life. What could
possibly go wrong? The blood moon, for example,
thought to be evil; the relentless sun, blazing on.
And is it so, my dear, that our long-time quarrel
can be explained, if not understood? Your heat,
explosion, fire balanced by my cool, dark water?

~
Does it matter if we're present?
When a tree falls in the forest,
when a cow passes gas in a field,
if no one is gazing at the moon?
So much depends on human perception,
they say. I say: ask ants in the rotted log
of our windbreak if hearing matters;
ask the burrowing woodchuck underground
if it perceives smell; ask the black-gold oriole
belting its spring melody from our treetop
if moonlight helped it migrate to this place.

~

Some 400 billion years ago, a planetary explosion
created the moon. Luna, the Roman moon
goddess, rode across the sky in a silver chariot.
The Omaha people believe the sun and moon
quarreled, resulting in division: scatter or gather,
direct or follow, walk or sleep, light or dark.
Tonight, the moon at crescent with bright-eyed
Venus beside it could be my father, winking.
Little brown bats flap and swoop for bugs
as this wild acre exhales in the pale light.
I'm a better human breathing the moon.

The Moon, in Pieces
JAMES HARMS

I'm no longer sure
the threads stitching here
to there will hold, the moon
in pieces, snagged
in the holly tree's branches.
I watched it slip free of two
clouds tossed like tissues in the sky,
watched it skim the blue
distances of a late summer night,
a night filled with leftover light.
How will the moon
survive so much light, the cuts
and tears of the holly's sharp leaves?
The moon in pieces, just
slivers of silver rising
through branches, dragging
its soft light toward
a truer darkness, the there
that isn't certain anymore.
Here will have to do.
I listen to the threads give way.

Winter Moon
DIXON HEARNE

The cruel moon crawls across the winter sky
mocking life below with frigid daring.
Near-lifeless creatures stir and huddle
against the bracing winds,
baying, crying for kind reprieve.

Row houses, paint-bare and drooping,
push single columns into the night air.
Shapeless figures float past the windows
flickering with warmth and promise—

As the timeless orb stares down
from its perch in the changing sky,
resigned to its singular duty
to stay the course.

Drawing Down the Moon
KATHLEEN HELLEN

I missed it last night, the clouds wrestling,
the super moon extinguished in the earth's
rising storm, the tv, Internet, losing precious
signal. I mirror everything in blackness black
as all our failures, the battered, densely cratered
basin of our darkness, the forces lasting, locked.
At any minute, though, I can make the fish leap
from the sea. I can take myself at speed of thought
like astronauts who've landed, roving landscapes
of maria, this little boat of mine adrift from earth's
umbilical, breaking off from all the roiling kettles,
the battles brute. Death-flagged. I pull at tides
from where I used to be, at polar caps, the coastlines.
As heart excites, the earth rises. Spectacular and full.
Someone, somewhere, suddenly turns on the light.

Moon Watching
LOU ELLA HICKMAN, I.W.B.S.

eclipse
annulus   ring of light
thin as my grandmother's wedding band
i wear now as a nun   the moon's small sister
how like the dark center
my life
surrounded with light i cannot see
but i know is there

2016: the year of the strange moons

omens perhaps . . .
the moon casts her nets as she has always done
        pulling oceans
            pulling our bodies' hidden seas
                dredging up our deepest fears

fairy tale

the moon's silence is the singing no one hears
in the story of the lonely gypsy
swirling around a fire called earth

Brown Bodies Swaying
ANGELA JACKSON-BROWN

Brown bodies cast strange moon shadows
as they hang like broken down dolls on
hilltops much like Golgotha.
The swaying of their bodies speaks volumes
of the state of affairs yet no one likes to listen
to loud whispers – the only sounds those bodies
can make.

Those bodies tell tales. Ancient tales of survival
when the moon was their only guide. Now, the
moon betrays them. Subverts the light it is casting
on them now – their final moment. That moon
is a liar. The hope she once had to guide them to
Freedom Land was all an illusion. Even if they could
call down the goddess Yemoja...even if she could promise
them their crucifixion is nothing like that other one...even
if she could promise to protect their women, men, boys
and girls, she would be a lying, dark ghost passing through
the midnight hours when bodies do the most swinging.

Swing low, sweet chariot...there is no home. Come by here
my lord...and do what? Bear witness to the killing, the
mutilation of collective legacies? Remember, when they die
all life stops. Their loins will forever be revoked,
so the promise they were destined to fill gets washed away
in the moonlight.

So I say, burn the bodies when they are done with their sadistic
moonlit dance. You should also pray that the ancestors
are hovering in the atmosphere in a benevolent mood, ready to catch
those ashes and pack them into their mouths, their eyes, their ears,
leaving no residue of these Queens and Kings who had to die
under the light of the moon.

Mooncalf
TIM KAHL

The moon is made up of whatever hit the earth.
It carries itself in the sky as a token of conflict.
It chases me as I sprint across the mesa asphalt
scrolling past the mesquite and creosote.
Yesterday a swarm of bees stung a dozen
worshippers at a mosque in Phoenix. They flew in
from the south through the open doors
enraged by something I can't grasp.
Later this evening I will drive into the Mojave,
stop at Barstow, and battle the traffic lights.
I will dream the confused play of the *nafs*,
the unruly horse of my mind that I must steer
to the north where my dwelling is expecting me.
I am mooncalf, a born fool with grit under his
fingernails impossible to rinse off. I am
guided by the moon at my back as I stand—
four abandoned walls in the scrubland.
I motor past Mockingbird Wash, past Old Camp Wash,
past Iron Wash, past Coyote Wash, past Ogata Wash
into the blowing dust area. I flash across
Astrid Wash, Manzanita Wash, past the exhibit
of ten thousand horseshoes and the mechanical
zoo. Tonight I ride with my windows rolled
down and shout my *shahadah* at the moon,
confident in its power over my decisions.
The road ahead must make me believe,
my head buzzing like an angry bee.
I bring my steel and glass steed speeding
through the sand, trying not to steal a glance
at my attention machines that pull down
images from the heavens. I fail to stay
completely focused, yet I hold the beast
to its forward progress. I scoot under
the overpass, the interstate ahead littered
with signs, but to this stubborn German
every step forward is also a retreat
from what is left behind.

A History of the Moon as It Sheds Itself Toward Full

GEORGE KALAMARAS

So the hound dogs cried out, bayed at it, begged it to bleed.

*

Once, at the height of a rare, second pregnancy, the moon—in secret—confided it didn't quite understand how time could ever be separated into *once*, or how there could be a unilateral direction of *in*, or the division, even, of color into *blue*.

*

He told me Michelangelo and Galileo were buried there, in the Franciscan Basilica di Santa Croce, across from one another. And, in between, remnants of the moon's gauze.

*

I walked out onto the back porch, crickets singeing the night with cruel moon-glow rubbed from their groins. The moon, bobbing in the waves of the backwoods pond. There it came over me. Into me. *Unto* me. Sliding slantwise through my throat.

*

Oh, there it is now in the shape of a possum. Marsupial pouch birthing its own white bloat. No wonder the bluetick coonhound keeps crawling toward it all light long.

*

If you ask the moon what the moon is, it will likely hide behind a cloud.

*

For many years, we knew of sixteen moons orbiting Jupiter. Now, another twenty-three have been discovered. *We are searching for names for them all*, said the shaman. *Here, dribble a little saliva onto this sacred cloth—this skunk hide—and see where it lands. Whether we should name each moon black or white, or something indistinct at the root—there—between hair follicles.*

*

In "The History of the Moon as it Mourns the Body of Meng Chiao," the Indiana poet wrote about hound dogs—as if the T'ang Dynasty poured through the moon, entering an Indiana cornfield, and coming out centuries later as magnolia-tinted lightning bugs the dogs longed to capture in the heartache of their throat.

*

In *A Very Brief History of the Moon*, the book contained twenty-eight sections, each composed of twenty-eight sentences, each twenty-eight words long. Then a storm came. A big storm. A little storm. And it rained. And the book was washed away.

*

I know, said the moon to no one in particular. *It gets lonely up here too.*

*

The woman walked down to the shore, cupped the waves in her hand, and drank pieces of what she would later say was herself, splintered there—white—in the frosted, frothy salt. *Are we water? Are we salt? Are we nothing but what the moon throws away of itself, day after day after it is full?*

*

Yes, said the moon. *We are all that and more.*

*

If we could speak, howled the hounds, baying at it night after night as it began to grow again, *we'd say we are not angry with you. No one could possibly be angry with you. We just want to hold you and—like you—be both up there and down here at once.*

The Missing Sock
DAVID KIRBY

You've searched everywhere: the washing machine, the couch.
Your wife says, you look like a boy with a stolen comic book

stuffed down his pants, and you say, No, I've just lost my sock.
Have you seen it? Maybe it's hidden among the other things, these

underpants, perhaps, or a shirt. Don't look for it! she says. Think how
lucky you are. You know what the philosophers say: everything

is material, even your distress. You have a new relationship with
that sock. There's something between you and it that doesn't exist

anywhere else in this world. Wouldn't you rather have that than
some stupid sock? Come to the window—the buildings are in ruins,

the city is turning to smoke, an ancient sea washes the streets.
Isn't all this better than a sock? And you say, Yes, yes,

I see. But what about the other sock? What am I to do with it?
In the sky, the moon crumbles – look, she says, it's turning into stars.

Oblivion
BRIAN JERROLD KOESTER

Over the cliff
five constellations of nymphs
reflect on a crystal sea

the crickets are screaming
their worship
of the moon

the moon refuses to hear me
my naked foot finds
sharp flint

the crystal breaks
my body   then melts
to take my blood

above   the nymphs whirl
like flowers that shine and speak
only of breezes

my voice goes to bleed
in a spiral
shell

A Litany of the Moon
PHILIP C. KOLIN

You birthed time's twin
blackening night by hiding

behind storms or
peeking through zany clouds.

But you also rouse the morning
into consciousness

and open the rooms of the sky
for lyrics and lyres

holding antiquity's memories,
and a museum for today's Argonauts.

You can speak the language of whispers
or proclaim the terror of an eclipse.

Half-heartedly you flirt with mountains
or slink down to cozen

oceans, dizzying them
into rushing rhapsodies.

You burn blood red
in the heat of the desert.

But you can bring the Eucharist
on a paten of alchemical gold

or play the courtesan
powdering your faces, manicuring

your nails, and fragrancing
the air with wisps of wildwood.

Like a gypsy in a caravan
of wobbling wheels

you tell fortunes but are eager
to escape any destination

that can be pinned down
on a map.

You are fantasy's
last frontier.

Moon Shadows
TED KOOSER

All night the moon was a lamp held steady
while an oak, alone on the crusted snow,
composed a long letter, thoughtfully forming
each word in the copperplate script
of its shadows. From a window halfway up
the stairs I watched it at work, the pale blue
airmail stationery smoothed and waiting
and the sentiments coming so slowly
that I grew impatient and climbed up to bed.
And I fell asleep wondering to whom
the tree might have been writing, and why,
and when I awoke the sky was gray
and cold, the sun hidden in clouds,
and the tree was just standing there,
reaching up into a few scattered snowflakes
then beginning to fall, not trying to catch them,
but letting them slip through its branches,
and the letter, whatever its message, was gone.

Path of Totality
BILL LAVENDER

corona like
fur around
the hole

what you don't
believe in
starts to howl

October Moon on the Lake
SYDNEY LEA

Not another poem about a stunning moon!
It won't be me who writes it.
I've heard the clichés, I've seen that shine so often,
there's nothing more to mean,
to see or say. And yet at that you ought to behold

this pair of night-time loons,
for instance, paddling through a riffled band of light
the moon has deftly laid
from that far shore to this. There may be more to come,
probably more to be told,

even more to signify. It's just that I,
feeling awkward, oblique, can't figure
how or what or why, no matter that now I consider
the cavortings over the sky
to my east of that trio of swallows, who might have returned to their holes,

twilight turning to dark,
to wherever they go after they've played themselves out.
They would have done so, no doubt,
had the moon under which they caper not been so immense,
so vivid, so candid, so bold.

The Big Orange Ball
PHILIP L. LEVIN

Five-years-old, lying on a blanket
On a small hill in the park
Far from the lights of our small town
When life was slower, and people liked to sit around
And watch the stars.
Mama beside me, humming a tune,
Daddy, with his thermos of coffee,
Listening to the frogs and crickets and nightbird songs.
The darkness haunted by
Light released hundreds of years ago
And billions of miles away.
Until, creeping over the treetops
The moon,
So huge it took two hands spread apart to reach the edges.
"Harvest Moon," my mother whispered.
"Wolf Moon," my father said.
Casting eerie ghost shadows on the ground
And awe in a young boy's heart.
Watching it rise ever higher, until the glow
Faded into dreams.
Sixty years later
Taking a grandson fishing and camping
In a dwindling wilderness,
Yet still far enough from big-city lights
To sit on a blanket, looking over the river, to the woods
Where a big orange ball makes its appearance
As it has every month, year after year,
Delighting five-year-old boys.

Maria Luna
MICHAEL A. LOFARO

Lying mirror, no virtue left to see
Gazes back interminably.
Ancient cataracts venerate
Fairy tale superstition
Pockmark memory, dreams convert reality.
Blind faith splotches views
Cratered younger self
Spirits rise, shine
More real than fact
Less true than legend.
Delusions new and old wax before
Reflection full but unheeded.

Two Nights
PETER MAKUCK

Last night a full moon
Bright and blazing through curtains
Would not let me sleep

Made me moody all day long,
Phyllis trying to draw me out.

Tonight at dinner
Between us sharp words bring down
An early darkness,

Make us leave the house to walk
The live-oak path to the beach.

Before we get there
A huge blood moon rises above
The black wall of trees

Has us stop for a long look
While crickets stitch up the day.

Silver Moon
PAUL MARIANI

Old moon rising over the Hotel David,
silvering the storied streets of Jerusalem.
Holy city, alleluia! Holy city.
Adolescent moon waving seaward beyond
Key West, glittering the palm-swayed beaches.
Acetylene moon, processing past Paterson's
brick silk mills as they drowsed
in the evening air, half aware of the steady
roar of the Great Falls, where we played among
the rusting iron fences when we were children.

Drunken moon, that night I drove my Beta
Sigma brothers through the Bronx streets
home to their apartments, swerving left, right,
left as I sang some inane insane song, and—
thanks to you, Henry, my watchful bulldog
Guardian Angel—have lived to talk about it.

Somnolent moon high over El Capitan, where
once a grizzly snuffled outside our cabin,
the kids thank God asleep. Moon higher
still over the Wilbur Cross Parkway,
forming a refulgent silver lake as we drove
north toward Hartford and beyond.

Brother moon, Br'er Moon, tangled
in a briar patch of clotheslines, an acrid sweetness
of baked tar coating the buckled roof
of my long lost crumbling brownstone tenement
which once faced the beckoning diamond lights
of the Chrysler. Antediluvian moon, moon
older than Moses, older than Ashurbanipal,
than Adam even, you, the lesser light the Lord
created on the fourth day, silvering the earth.

Moon, dear moon, the comfort you bring
each time I catch you as you slowly process past,
left to right, but steadier than I was then,
royal moon choired by katydids, or peeking
through the glittered winter ice. Catch you, ah!,
whenever I climb the creaking stairs in darkness.
In truth, you seem to look down and wink at me
through the stained glass window when I reach
the landing with its giant potted eucalyptus.
Oh I know that at the core you are a floating
rock pockmarked with shadow craters, half
of you forever hidden in darkness. I know too
there are even black and white images taken
by men—all of them gone now, such is our fate,
our common fate, even for those who reach
for stars, and who, half floating in their awkward
necessary lifelines, dream of touching you.

Moon, old moon, dear moon, I beg you
answer me when I call out to you,
as I have from the eerie hospital bed,
or over the dashboard of my car, or from
the north room where my love is sleeping now,
here next to me, as she has for fifty years
and more, constant companion, as you
have been, old moon, silvering on, alleluia.

It's Never a Small Problem
TOD MARSHALL

Because the moon is always many things—awful judge with a walleye gaze
or shy fish at the bottom of a stagnant pond or light and air compressed through
a cylinder when the valves respond to rocker arms, pistons shove,
sparks ignite the car down the road, seventy on sand and gravel
that feels like a gritty mouthful of that sweet thing as a kid you dropped
but stooped over to pick up, lick clean, because some things you have to have—
matters not.
                Light on the hood shimmers faded paint into your own pond,
a glittery blue that dulls when you think you hear a kick against the quarter panel,
stubborn struggling duct-taped in the trunk. There's nothing in there,
you tell yourself. You have driven the dirt roads until dust on the dash
   will hold the letter O,
and still nothing comes together, moon and guilt, ruthless beauty and the small
mechanical things that you believe move the world. Consider the composition of
shadows,

the darkness beyond the ditch purple-black with a smell close to lilac,
but burnt, unlike anything living, the odor of a bell that's never been struck.

Blood Moon
KAREN McPHERSON

I didn't write about it when it happened
last fall, when that body in full perigee
crossed into Earth's long shadow and filled up
with blood—how it was eclipsing all
terrestrial observations, turning all
poets' tides. My page stayed discreet as a star-
speckled, new moon sky.

But now, this week, I see it's growing
full again—not gravid hanging low, but rather high
and thin, indifferent. And while the nights
are clear, the days are heavy with catastrophe.
And while we are in its shadow, we know that
somewhere there's another moon
choking on its blood.

Moonmen Land in the Okefenokee
PETER MEINKE

Moonman2 sound the alarm we
are stuck in a swamp area
the air is noxious we have spotted
unidentified striding objects
it would be difficult for us
to slide in this apparently hostile
terrain geophysical characteristics
green brown mud rain
the air heavy hard to breathe
this morning ffrlq ventured out
at the end of a rope we almost lost
her the air we repeat is foul
our fuel is low likewise hope I
don't think we can get out more
uso's approaching they may
have some intelligence they
are not green they look
afraid and dangerous I
think they mean us harm now
I think we are seen sound
the alarm sou . . .

When the Moon Opened My Life
CARYN MIRRIAM-GOLDBERG

I was expecting it, even willing it.
I leaned out the second story window
to get a better view through the branches
now that the troublesome leaves had dropped.
I was a child in a city, but I knew, like all animals
with their dewy eyes, what an enchantment was.
The moon exhaled rings of pink light dissolving
into darkness filled with more stars, more moons too.

Maybe it opened my life years earlier,
before I had words to catch what I saw: the moon
watching the sun in slivers, halves, orbs
I would return to my whole life, once from the middle
of a windy field, walking up a slight incline
to catch up with my friends and the car.

Or from the passenger window of a warming car
where I listened to women singing in another language
on the radio, the contractions already hurting so much,
but there was no place to go but this seat,
where I waited for my husband to drive me.
The moon would wait with me, or wake me many times,
a flash light in the dark that made me unzip a sheer tent
and squat barefoot on the gravel, looking up, shivering,
but grateful to be so cold and alive while the rest
of the family slept right through that big noisy light.

Just last week, I stood on the brink of a narrow beach
and watched the moon turn the pages of the ocean,
wave by wave, far from home, but the moon has a way
of dissolving ideas like "home" or "away." It's just
the moon, the one that returns me each time it opens
the door another inch, lifts the weathered window frame.

Moon and Stars in Synchrony
ROBERT MORGAN

Arable: the word suggests both light
and playfulness, the mixing in
of air and soil, enriching dirt
with carbon and with nitrogen,
the opening up of one horizon
where seed can find the moisture and
the womb to germinate and thrive
on salts and other minerals.
The term itself derives from Latin,
the Roman word for plow, the point
which spreads the furrow to receive
the seed, exposing humus to
both sunlight and the atmosphere.
The Cayuse said they knew it was
a sacrilege to rip the soil,
to torture land to bring about
an artificial crop the earth
had neither sought nor valued. They
would rather starve in winter months
until the salmon came again.
But working with the earth in a
collaboration is perhaps
a satisfaction unsurpassed
in this our mortal sphere and span.
To scratch the soil, to turn the dirt,
to stir the soil to be receptive,
and fertile and cooperative,
with moon and stars in synchrony
with swing of seasons, tilt of earth's
as much as we accomplish in this
our period on the planet's surface.

Medical Moons
MARY MURPHY

Despite several studies, it has never been proven there is an increase in hospital admittances or medical emergencies during full moons. While the word lunacy is associated with lunar, this dates back to ancient times and the fear of evil spirits and witches taking possession of human souls.

The medical workers went back in the Emergency Room, after their break outside in the cold, drinking coffee under the bright Harvest Moon, away from the stench and sounds of patients' illnesses.

Full moons, especially during the Spring or Fall, allow extra time for laborers.

A veteran in the mental holding room is banging the walls and screaming—"Run! Oh God! Run!"

A tale from Chinese mythology is of a rabbit on the moon forever pounding with a mortar and pestle the elixir of life.

The old woman looks at the corpse of her dead husband. "The first time he did it was on our honeymoon. The doctor back then told me all I had to do was relax."

The legend tells that a rabbit was placed in the moon by the gods to show the world its sacrifice: it had nothing to give a starving peasant but the bitter grass it chewed every day. The creature in pity threw itself into the camp fire as an offering.

A five year old boy has adult bite marks all over his body; X-rays show a severe brain bleed. His parents are telling the police officer, "We just couldn't wake him up from his nap. He's usually very happy and gets right up."

A Harvest Moon looks like a full moon for several nights, but it is an illusion.

A teenager from the car accident lies in the trauma room, his sheets freshly changed so his parents will not see the severity of his injuries and the amount of blood lost. He is unresponsive as they keep screaming his name and ask for him to squeeze their fingers.

The Harvest Moon rises just as the sun is setting.

In Afterglow
ROBERT NAZARENE

The moon has been curdling. Above her,
a lamina of pale tumors glint in the sky—
her bedsheet. She is dripping sweat. All
is stethoscope cold and silent. It's a change
from gazing down at lovers in canoes.
They've gone and done it. The earth below—
spread out like an autopsy.

Eagle
NICK NORWOOD

*Jettisoned from the Command Module
on 21 July 1969 at 23:41UT (7:42 PM EDT)
Impact site unknown*
  —NASA

Hangs, a tin can with legs,
above the moon's pallor,
floats down like a feather
to plant her feet in chalk.

Out of her, the first man
steps, also the second,
to hop about and speak
brave words about the first steps

of men. She squats, remains
womb, sanctuary, home,
until it's time for their
return, to reunite

with *Columbia.* Then
her frail rockets fire just
enough to lift them, leave
that gleaming desolate

soil to which she, lone,
abandoned, will fall back,
crumbling, a heap of foil
cracked open like an egg.

On Looking at the Night Sky
LINDA PASTAN

Let's say the moon is just
a keyhole in the sky,

that if I put my eye to it
I'd see whole galaxies

of mothers in aprons, mustached
fathers, friends— angels now

spinning like so many planets
and clothed in light.

Which is to say that age
sits heavily on my shoulders

as I distract myself
with heavenly nonsense.

But it's the morning sky I'll miss,
the sun coming up

pure spectacle at the window,
steeping the earth in color.

It's beauty I'll miss: snow
etching my windshield,

dew varnishing each flower.
Though darkness too

is beautiful, I tell myself.
And always the moon.

Diana Expectant
JOSEPH PEARCE

Above all shadows rides the sun,
Beyond the gloom, the knell of doom;
And, with the sun, another one
The darkened loom cannot entomb.

An orb of white reflected light;
Radiant womb, celestial bloom;
Elevated host, bridal white,
Mirroring the awaited groom.
A chaste, unchastened hecatomb.

And so, in veiled vestal livery,
Diana heralds dawn's delivery.

The Full Moon of July
MARGE PIERCY

It's the thunder moon. Great
stone wheels are driven across
the sky. The moon is hiding
behind them but egging on
the storm as it blunders over.

Jagged stalks of lightning
fork down. We fear them
wishing the storm would pass
without damage. The wind
pushes against the shingles

rattles windows, turns trees
insideout like ruined umbrellas.
Streams run down the street.
Suddenly it's gone out to sea.
Only a drip drip on the roof.

The moon comes sailing through
the wreckage of spent clouds.
Every drop is mercury's silver
glittering on bush and tree. Air
is washed clean till it shines.

We fear and need the thunder
moon, ending drought, sucking
life from apple and rabbit. Every
tree raises fingers of praise.
We're wet and saved again.

A Little Light
KEVIN RABAS

How easily we can see
  past the solar system
at night, other stars, like eyes,
  watching, watching us
in darkness, and the moon, close,
  knows even we
shed a little light.

Long Marriage (Moon)
DOUG RAMSPECK

And if the moon is turning through the decades,
rolling across the sky's mud, this must be the geography

of memory, each wheel with its circumnavigations,
its myopia of clouds. We wake most mornings

to the sacred music of the birds, or then it is winter
and the ice along the river becomes a first skin, a layering

or a palimpsest. Or what if we sip our coffee
for a decade in the back yard, or the moon is impaled

in the limbs of a willow? In certain dreams the wagon
is rising and falling on the prairie waves, and my wife's

breaths are rising and falling as we sleep. What is the meaning
of a wheel that spins? Or what if we grow mired in the mud,

so stall? Doesn't the dark hall of the night enclose us?
Don't we still lean our shoulders into the passage?

Moon Headlines Ghazal
DIANE RAPTOSH
(composed entirely of headlines culled from various news sources)

Aim at the Stars and End Up on the Moon
How Bright is the Earth as Seen from the Moon?

Moon Rock Rolls Inside the Air and Space Museum
Can We See the Earth's Rotation from the Moon?

Pie in the Sky and the Moon in June
Arizona State Students to Create Life on the Moon

Jeff Bezos Smooths a Path toward Lunar Deliveries
Are Plans Being Made to Brew Beer on the Moon?

Deep Space Entices Upstarts and Mainstays
You Cannot Reach the Moon in Your Mercedes

Sorry Millennials, the 'Pink Moon" Won't Be Pink
Moon Jae-in, South Korea's Candidate for Prez, a Pinko?

Bibles Flown to Moon Stir Ownership Dispute
Entrance to Underground Cave Found on the Moon

New Film Shows How NASA 'Faked Apollo Mission'
Backyard Bass Take Bait Behind the Moon

Massive Asteroid to Safely Cruise Past Earth
How Can We Tell When Objects Clip the Moon?

Moon and Ahn Give Their All to Attack Each Other
Flood Warning Issued for Moon River

Holy Temple Planned for the Moon's South Pole
You: Part Owner of the Moon and Stars by Law. No Joke

The Plan to Nuke the Moon and Other Cold War Plots
We Know the Pink Moon's Coming But What's That?

A Waning Crescent

(For Addie Mae Collins, Cynthia Wesley, Denise McNair, Carole Robertson, Johnny Robinson, and Virgil Ware)[1]

JOSEPH ROSS

On 9/15/1963 the moon over Birmingham, Alabama was a waning crescent, only 6% visible.

You were a waning
crescent, the barest
of slivers in the darkest
night Alabama knows.

You were a trace
of light
these children could not
see.

They each slept
under your curving
back, unaware of the
tides to come.

You were a silent wound
in the stabbed sky.
You said nothing.

You should have been
a warning to us all
on such a lightless night
as 1963.

---

[1] On Sunday, September 15, 1963, in Birmingham, Alabama, racial violence claimed the lives of six children. Two were shot at random, Johnny Robinson by a white police officer, and Virgil Ware by a white teen. The other four, Addie Mae Collins, Cynthia Wesley, Denise McNair, Carole Robertson were killed in the 16th Street Baptist Church bombing.

The bomber, the cop,
the boy, the bricks, the bullets,
they did not ask
for your light.
They did not need
your protection.

But we do.
We need to see.
We need to be
the waning, the waxing,
and the warning.

New Moon at Race Point
JASON ROUSH

The Provincetown airport runway beacon
sweeps Cape Cod's seascape with white light
every two seconds like the heartbeat of the world,

catches the frame of the ranger station, with its lone
round blue safety light in an attic window,
the solitary eye of the afterworld.

I sit alone in my parked car, its shadow thrown
against the intermittent dunes, and my own
shadow's there inside it, gazing faceless

through the windshield at my familiar facelessness.
I remember when a friend walking the beach
here at midnight found a dead body in the dark,

under the stars, a gun lying next to it in the sand.
The new moon tonight feels like it knows me,
a hidden compass point in missing constellations.

Four Moon Haiku

(For Harriett Tubman)

SONIA SANCHEZ

I.

Picture a woman
walking southern landscapes
burning with moons...

II.

Picture her
singing red moons
surprising life...

III.

Picture her moon
bent legs dancing inside
freedom's guitar...

IV.

Picture a woman
moving in winter black
bringing summer moons...

Sixteen Moon Haiku
SONIA SANCHEZ

1.

Can my eyes
withstand the beauty of
this August moon?

2.

O Moon
shimmering in the night
ambushed by stars!

3.

Here she comes
this new moon
poaching the sky.

4.

The night
chanted complicated
moons.

5.

O moon shining
your autumnal glow
summer has gone.

6.

This autumn moon
a flash of
wild orange.

7.

The morning
moving in short breaths
discarded moon.

8.

I see your
half moon eyes
watching me dance...

9.

O full moon
rounding this vast
corner of darkness.

10.

Moon O red moon
Why do you make
me cry?

11.

O moon
I taste the secret corners
of your breath...

12.

Night
breaking into the
color of moonlight.

13.

The moon
swimming in a
sea of blue.

14.

I...born
in an avalanche
of burnt moons.

15.

I say a prayer
to the moon rinsing
my eyes.

16.

My eyes shudder
in this blue night
of red moons.

The Moon Ten Times
PAT SCHNEIDER

After Wallace Stevens'
"Thirteen Ways of Looking at a Blackbird"

1.
O round, cool face of forever
float free
for me

2.
Saucer without a teacup
without the tyranny
of tea

3.
Owl eye without a pupil
blind
to contradiction

4.
My white balloon
has lost its string
and me

5.
Round, open mouth
of the goddess
of light

6.
The night sky's
exclamation
Oh!

7.
Puppeteer
of tides
rock the shore of the world

8.
Bright Frisbee
the dog star lost
in the night

9.
Perfect pearl
crown of cornfields
and night watchmen's hair

10.
Window
between here
and there

I No Longer Have the Moon
MARTHA SERPAS

I no longer have the moon
I've laid it on the inky Gulf
next to my virginity
a rumpled half slip on the bedspread

a smoky wasp's nest of all the eggs I sent
on their way (thirty-five years of half-me's)
on my way to having you—
this absence! our new new moon

The Refiner
MARLEY STUART

My brother has the phases of the moon
etched on his wedding ring. It's subtle,
something you wouldn't see unless you knew
it was there. He keeps the secret

pressed to his palm as he flips wheels of cheese
or checks the progress of mold. In the caves,
he gets to work, developing his craft.

He's been able to reinvent himself
more than once so far—line cook, pastry chef,
finally, affineur—so the moon makes sense.
It seems to change, but keeps its essence pure.

My brother's husband chose for his ring
a white stone, the moon their language
in a world they've built. Each was born
a girl and came to light a man, undoing

the false skin of first life. No mystery
they found each other—blood pulls at blood
by design, to make stray pieces whole.

My brother labors in the cheese caves
longer each day and steps into the pasture a man
restored, his eyes flashing clean and white.

Benediction for a Caribbean Moon
VIRGIL SUÁREZ

(After Charles Baudelaire)

Once, just once, the sky breaks open and the birds spill
outward from the clouds, falling like black words, a silken

avalanche, swooned like abandon, a young woman meets
her lover in the shadows of her balcony. He has brought

her a single hibiscus flower, still bleeding its milky juice;
she clips the flower to her moon-glow caught hair,

her hand clutches his against her breast, a burst of flame,
iridescent as a star, under the ceiba tree's somber shade,

the Cuban parrot chatters, proud-footed on the bough,
its bright eyes turned to the balcony, where wind carries

the notes of a *decima guajira* from a bar across the street,
a familiar tune for lovers, lights blink between the trees,

enough desire to burn their silhouettes against moonlight.

Last Day on Inishark Island
MARY SWANDER

High tide and now—with no natural
harbor, the moon was all on Inishark,
how and when it was safe to push off
and venture away from the ancient rock
that jutted out of the Atlantic Ocean.
On fishing days, the men winched their
currachs over the cliff and into the sea,
slipping out alone in boats of hide and cones.
They crossed themselves, praying
their rosaries, pulling back on the oars,
their water-slapped faces nodding
to the forces that took three Lacey boys—
a syzygy all their own—
down in the terrible drowning,
only one ever to be found,
washed up against the shore,
They crossed themselves, staring back
at their homes receding in the distance:
the cottages and farmland where
year after year their ancestors
had grazed sheep in the pastures
and on the steep bluffs, had planted
potatoes in ridges and stored them in mounds
with hopes they would last the winter,
where St. Leo's Church filled once a month,
with men leaning against the wall
and women squatting down on the little
three-legged stoops they'd carried in,
with the priest giving a blessing
of the boats, the crops, and the animals,
for a bountiful year, for good health
for all and good weather when ill.
With no doctor, no phone, no lights,
the sun and moon were all,

shining down on the island and sea,
but no waxing was enough.
To signal help, a bonfire on the beach,
the flames rising high enough to see
on Inisbofin, the next island,
where men might row out to help,
if the wind, moon and tides were right.
On Inishark, a family might be without flour,
sugar, or tea for six weeks during the winter,
sun and moon hidden behind the clouds.
A man might lie for three days
and three nights in writhing pain before
his appendix burst and he took his place
in the graveyard, bones sinking into the sand.

So God willing, Sunday mornings saw
families in currachs on the waves,
three miles to Bofin to Mass at St. Colman's,
to the post office for the week's mail,
to the shop for store-bought biscuits.
What a delight, what a treat,
to be heading into a good harbor
where all the invaders had landed—
the Vikings to the Brits—and though
they had made a prison of the castle,
in the end, even Cromwell hadn't lasted.
What had? The rockrose wedged into the granite.

The corncrake scratching out
its call among the nettles and yellow dock,
the moonbeams bouncing off the water.
And now, on this day, the fishermen row
their final voyage from Shark to Bofin,
the last time their family squeezes
into the boat, mothers and children
with the sun and moon and all they own:
kettles, old bed frames, hens in baskets,
geese in sacks, a stack of hay,
straw brooms and string-tied suitcases,
a dark brown cat in a blackened cooking pot

with the lid half tied down,
rakes and scythes, calves tied
to the currach to swim to their new home,
the little collie dog, at the stern.
With no doctor, no resident priest
with cotton balls and oil,
no phone nor lights, no chance
for the children to go to school,
or know a different, better life, they set out,
the whole island at once for Bofin,
then on to Cleggan on the mainland.
They turn and wave at old Tommy Lacey,
the spirits of two of his sons still circling above,
disappeared into the clouds,
hidden behind the waning of the crescent.
Tommy stands in his doorway,
refusing to budge, refusing to leave,
despite the priest's begging and pleas.
He alone will stay where his boys
went down. Shark was where he was born.
He built his house with his own hands.
Now. Go on lads, go.
he waves back, the boats drifting out.
One by one, the islanders lose sight of him—
only the smoke from the peat fire
rising into the air from the chimney.
The night presses down,
the stars and moon his all.
The fire in his hearth goes out.
In the morning, Tommy sets two places
at the table—knives, forks, spoons
good china plates and cups.
He makes a pot of tea, puts out butter,
sugar, brown bread and marmalade,
says the blessing before meals.
Then he waits for the tides and
the moon to align, the wind to calm,
and he rows out one last time
away from the island into the sea.

Lunatic Pantoum

(For Marie Ponsot)

LEONARD A. TEMME

The moon is my friend   The moon is my enemy
The moon is the shape shifter shifting its arc
of night skyshine reflected inside me
folded in the safe danger of dark.

The moon is the shape shifter shifting its arc
to recast the common place as mystery.
Folded in the safe danger of dark
I embrace what I cannot see.

To recast the common place as mystery
the moon's reflected self projects its pale grace.
I embrace what I cannot see,
yet I see what I cannot embrace.

The moon's reflected self projects its pale grace.
It is my enemy.   It is my friend.
Yet I see what I cannot embrace,
the twilight sun where shade and shadow blend.

It is my enemy.   It is my friend.
It is the twin side of dark and light,
the twilight sun where shade and shadow blend.
(The terror hidden there is all delight.)

It is the twin sides of dark and light,
of night skyshine reflected inside me
(The terror hidden there is all delight.)
The moon is my friend   The moon is my enemy.

Barry's Moon
JAMES TORRENS, S.J.

In the night of your confinement
   when you are not let out for air
you take up your colors and brush
   and utter the world within you.

Its moon takes up most of the sky,
   a bulging globe in a black square.

It shines through a midnight tree,
   leafless, with imploring arms,
   which a golden band entwines.

Your earth, purple or green,
   does not fail of flowers,
   three-petaled and red.

The sun may have smitten you by day,
   but the moon, its pale mirror,
   will not smite from the dark, Barry.

Even the Moon Must Have Troubles
JACQUELINE ALLEN TRIMBLE

Must sometimes climb off its golden swing
drown its sorrows in moon pies
or throw back bottle after bottle
of moonshine with the boys.
At some point it stalks a quiet street
moons the ladies and local preacher,
throws its beams indiscriminately
through every window in town,
howling, as it has seen wolves do,
at the old man who lives inside it
and feasts on green cheese. It marvels
at its round reflection on the lake,
joins a group of revelers, sings loudly
around a campfire, *I see the moon,*
the moon sees me. The moon sees the one
I want to see. "Lunatic," the locals call
as if they have never been moonstruck,
have never mooned over Ala
or Diana, never, not once, lost themselves
to loneliness and lunacy in a lover's arms
beneath its harvest light.

Ultimately
SUE BRANNAN WALKER

(Γράφω)[1]

The moon was full, and Mama called on the phone. "Q,"
she said (short for Susie-Q), tonight's the night. As sure as God
made little green apples, it's coming. I know you're about to the
end of your row waiting almost nine months, but mercy
me, the waiting is over, child. Over.

6:41 a.m. Moon surge—and the doctor said, "he's peeing on me."
I was one proud mama, my boy coming into the world
like that, making his presence known right from the get-go, while
my moon-struck husband dialed L.A. – Los Angeles, not L.A., Lower
Alabama to tell Grandma and Grandpa about their grandson
piddling on the doctor first thing he did.

Grandma was right about the moon's shenanigans;
she was a recognized diviner, an astrologer,
though not a selenographist[1]

After her second cup of joe, Granny phoned
and offered her condolences. She'd hoped for a girl
for "a daughter's a daughter all of her life," she said
"and a son is a son 'til he takes a wife."

"What did you name him?" Grandma said, sleep still stuck in her throat
mid-morning. "What you name the little fellow?"

    "Ulna."

    "What did you say?"

    "Ulna Hand. Ulna Hand."

    "That's a dern bone, ain't it?," Granny said. "Who ever heard of a
kid named after a bone!"

tik-tik boom, boom boom[2]

"Every name has a story behind it, every word, every letter, is delivered just like a baby," Ulna's daddy said. He was a college professor with a Ph.D.[3] and had studiously studied Derrida: "The name: *What does one call thus? What does one understand under the name of name? And what occurs when one gives a name?*"

"Little Ulna's going to be an orthopedic surgeon," his papa said. 'He's going to put the broken back together again. Heal them. And it's a scientific fact that the hand is the implement that sets human beings apart from every other species, at least that's the case up to the perilous times in which we live through all phases of the moon."[4]

LUNIC NOTATIONS
[1] Selenography is the study of the surface and physical features of the moon whereby selenographists' concern was mapping and naming the lunar maria, craters, and other features.

[2] Tik-tik boom is the opening Prelude, a solo piece, by drummer Billie Davies, in the musical composition, "Hand in Hand In The Hand Of The Moon." It is the intersection of two life-paths, that of Davies, a musician, and Serge Vandercam, a painter. It is a collaboration – a birthing of what is considered some of the most heartfelt music ever played.

[3] The hand has eight carpals. These small bones comprise the wrist area between the bones of the forearm and the phalanges, or fingers, of the hand. **The lunate** is one of these eight carpal bones. These carpals are arranged in two rows, and the lunate is located in the row closest to the radius and ulna. The name comes from the Latin word for moon, and the bone derives this name from its shape. It resembles that of a crescent moon.

[4] The word selenography is derived from the Greek deity, Σελήνη (Selene), and γράφω (graphō), meaning "I write."

Trigger Warning
SHANTI WEILAND

Children, you don't want
to hurt, to feel
the growth that stretches
all of us beyond what night
can comfort.

Night is no friend
to the old. The moon
hears our prayers
but does nothing.
How could it?

The young secure
their helmets tightly
around memories,
the fear of cracking
them open, the wound
of freedom.

Here is a story
I heard back
when my body
hummed like
a wasps' nest: Mother
Moon, curious
about the dark, cloaked
her bright body
and descended
to the bog where
vines and swamps
and all sorts of
problems pulled her
away from sky. No one
could function without
her.

Take heart, kids, the villagers
could not cry for the

orphans again, not one
more time, so they set out
on a journey, like the one
you're on now, and of course,
found themselves drawn
to the light, little dusty moths
fluttering around her
beautiful face. They lifted
the cloak, and her freedom
meant light and peace
for them.

But, as life goes, she still
pulls the cloak tight and
settles into the bog, now
and again, to remember
what makes her
the moon.

Children, it is only
on *those* nights
that we all
stay inside.

Icarus on the Moon
CAREY SCOTT WILKERSON

Icarus is a lunar impact crater that lies on the Moon's far side. It has a worn rim and a relatively wide inner wall. A small crater lies across the southern rim, and the side bulges outward slightly along the southwestern face. There is a disproportionately tall central peak located near the crater midpoint.
—Gazeteer of Planetary Nomenclature

Icarus landed on the Moon's dark side
and now believes himself part of a cosmic
charade designed to keep mythic failures
quiet and prevent them from reclaiming
the world as their own. Deep in his crater,
he relives versions of his own story:
plunging first into the Aegean Sea,
then diving straight through Victoria Falls,
splashing down in glasses of Chardonnay,
in backyard swimming pools, and in lovers'
last tears. Even as his father's voice warns
him against self-parody, his crater's
center peak pushes at a cloudless sky,
hangs in space waiting for the sun to rise.

Ten Impressions: Moon
JIANQING ZHENG

fall moonrise
a rowboat startles
waterfowls

      moonrise
      a crescent line of
      wave foam

autumn moon
a white Go stone snaps
onto the board

      oh! the moon's shadow
      has crept up the pine trees
      autumn deepens

out of woods
the hunter's moon
prowls closer

      bamboo flute—
      autumn moonlight
      gleaming white

cat yowling
there's the tangled moon
when I look out

      red moon watch
      peeling an orange
      while waiting

full moon
a light circle for clouds
to slide in and out

      Halloween night
      the live oak's gyrating limbs
      hold the moon

CONTRIBUTORS' NOTES

Ralph Adamo's most recent books are *Ever: Poems 2000-2014* (Lavender Ink/Dialogos Books) and *Waterblind: New and Selected Poems* (Portals Press, 2002). He teaches at Xavier University in New Orleans, where he edits *Xavier Review*. Winner of NEA and LEA Fellowships in Creative Writing, he is also editor of Everette Maddox's selected poems, and past editor of *New Orleans Review*

Alice J. Aldridge, an MBA and former CFO for two companies, is working on a book of poems about animals and healing. She is a lifelong Petal, Mississippi resident.

Maureen Alsop is the author of *Mirror Inside Coffin* (Cherry Grove Imprint), *Mantic* (Augury Books), *Apparition Wren* (Main Street Rag), *Later, Knives and Trees* (Negative Capability Press). Her book, *Apparition Wren* (Reyezuelo *Aparición*), was translated into Spanish by Mario Dominguez Parra. She lives on an island in the Coral Sea.

Ned Balbo recently published *Upcycling Paumanok* (Measure Press). He received a 2017 NEA translation grant for his version-in-progress of Paul Valéry's "La Jeune Parque." His next book *3 Nights of the Perseids* was selected by Erica Dawson for the 2018 Richard Wilbur Award. He currently teaches in the MFA program in creative writing and environment at Iowa State University.

Mary Jo Bang is the author of eight books of poems, including *A Doll for Throwing, Louise in Love,* and *Elegy,* which received the National Book Critics Circle Award. Her translation of Dante's *Inferno*, with illustrations by Henrik Drescher, was published by Graywolf Press in 2012. She's been the recipient of a Hodder Fellowship, a Guggenheim Fellowship, and a Berlin Prize Fellowship. She teaches creative writing at Washington University in St. Louis.

Frederick W. Bassett is a retired academic. His poems have appeared widely in anthologies and journals, including *Georgia Review, Illuminations, Negative Capability, Mudfish, Passager, Pembroke Magazine, POEM, Slant, The Cape Rock, Timberline Review, Yemassee,* and *Zone 3.* He has four books of poetry, the latest being *The Old Stoic*

Faces the Mirror. He also has two novels of a planned trilogy, *South Wind Rising* and *Honey from a Lion*. An Alabama native, he currently lives in Greenwood, SC.

Michael Bassett is a poet, philosopher, book lover, visual artist, and educator. He is the author of four poetry volumes, including *Hatchery of Tongues* (2014), as well as a children's book, *Batrocks and Greenie*. He lives in Savannah, Georgia.

Joseph Bathanti is former Poet Laureate of North Carolina (2012-14) and recipient of the 2016 North Carolina Award for Literature. He is the author of ten books of poetry, including *The 13th Sunday after Pentecost*, released by LSU Press in 2016. He's also the author of four books of fiction, and two books of nonfiction. Bathanti is Professor of Creative Writing at Appalachian State University and served as the 2016 Charles George VA Medical Center Writer-in-Residence in Asheville, NC.

Jill Peláez Baumgaertner is the author of four poetry collections; a textbook/anthology, *Poetry*; and *Flannery O'Connor: A Proper Scaring*, in addition to over forty essays, and has edited the poetry anthology *Imago Dei*. She has been a Fulbright scholar and is the winner of several poetry awards. She is Professor of English Emerita and former Dean of Humanities and Theological Studies at Wheaton College, where she served as Acting Provost. She currently serves as poetry editor of *The Christian Century*.

Jack B. Bedell is Professor of English and Coordinator of Creative Writing at Southeastern Louisiana University where he edits *Louisiana Literature* and directs the Louisiana Literature Press. His latest collections are *Elliptic* (Yellow Flag Press, 2016), *Revenant* (Blue Horse Press, 2016), and *Bone-Hollow, True: New & Selected Poems* (Texas Review Press, 2013). He has been appointed by Governor John Bel Edwards to serve as Louisiana Poet Laureate, 2017-2019.

Stephen Behrendt is George Holmes Distinguished University Professor of English at the University of Nebraska. He is an authority on British Romantic-era literature and culture as well as a founding member of the university's program in Interdisciplinary Nineteenth-Century Studies. He is also a widely published poet; his most recent book-length collection, *Refractions*, was published by Shechem Press (Spokane, WA) in late 2014.

Kris Bigalk is the author of the poetry collection *Repeat the Flesh in Numbers*. Her work has appeared in many literary magazines, including *Water-Stone Review*, *Paper Nautilus*, and *Cream City Review*. She serves as Director of Creative Writing at Normandale College.

John Bradley is the author of seven books of poetry and prose, his most recent *Erotica Atomica*, WordTech Edtions. He has had lunar tendencies most of his life.

Kim Bridgford is the director of Poetry by the Sea: A Global Conference, and editor of *Mezzo Cammin*. She is the author of nine books of poetry, including *Doll* and *Human Interest*. The recipient of grants from the Connecticut Commission on the Arts, the NEA, and the Ucross Foundation, she currently lives in the Fishtown area of Philadelphia. Her three-book project with visual artist Jo Yarrington, *The Falling Edge*, is forthcoming.

John J. Brugaletta is professor emeritus of English and comparative literature at California State University, Fullerton, where he edited *South Coast Poetry Journal* for ten years. He has published over 325 poems in 65 venues and has six collections of his poetry in print, the latest of which is *Peripheral Visions* (Negative Capability Press, 2017). X.J. Kennedy has called his selected poems "a vital contribution to American poetry."

Peter Neil Carroll's newest collections of poetry are *An Elegy for Lovers* (Main Street Rag, 2017) and *The Truth Lies on Earth* (Turning Point Press, 2017) as well as *Fracking Dakota: Poems for a Wounded Land*; and *A Child Turns Back to Wave: Poetry of Lost Places* which won the Prize Americana. His poems have appeared in print and online. He is currently Poetry Moderator for Portside.org and lives in northern California.

Kelly Cherry is the author of 27 books, 11 chapbooks, and 2 translations of classical drama. Her newest titles, published in 2017, are *Quartet for J. Robert Oppenheimer: A Poem*, *Beholder's Eye: Poems*, and *Temporium: Before the Beginning to After the End: Fictions*. Forthcoming in 2018 are *Men with Something to Say* (essays) and *Fault Lines: Poems*. A former Poet Laureate of Virginia, she has received a number of awards listed on her Wikipedia page.

Michael Chitwood's most recent collection, *Search & Rescue*, was published in 2018 by LSU Press. His work has appeared in *The Atlantic, Poetry, Threepenny Review* and numerous other publications.

Jeremy DeFatta has an M.A. in English from the Univ. of Southern Mississippi. His poetry has appeared in *Black Magnolias, Vineyards,* and *Flytrap Uprising*. He is co-owner / co-founder of Blue Spider Books, a monthly subscription service for coffee and used books. He currently works in an emergency room, where each day holds new lessons about life and death.

Will Dowd is a writer and artist from the Boston area. He earned a BA from Boston College, an MS from MIT, and an MFA in Creative Writing from New York University. His work has appeared in numerous places, including *Tin House* online, *LitHub, The Rialto, Post Road Magazine,* and NPR.org. His debut collection of lyric essays is *Areas of Fog* (Etruscan Press, 2017).

Mircea Dan Duta, Romanian born Czech poet, translator and film critic. His published work appears in *Landscapes, Flights and Dictations* (poetry - 2014), *Canned Quotes, Inferiority Complexes and Human Rights* (poetry - 2015), *Narrator and God* (2009 - film science & history), *Holocaust in Czech, Polish and Slovak Literature & Cinema* (2008 - film science & literary theory).

Stuart Dybek's most recent book *The Start of Something: Selected Stories of Stuart Dybek* (Jonathan Cape/Vintage) was published Fall 2017. His most recent collection of poems, *Streets in Their Own Ink* (FSG), appeared in 2015. He is the distinguished writer in residence at Northwestern University.

Martin Espada's latest collection of poems is *Vivas to Those Who Have Failed* (2016). Other books of poems include *The Trouble Ball* (2011), *The Republic of Poetry* (2006), and *Alabanza* (2003). He has received the Shelley Memorial Award, the PEN/Revson Fellowship and a Guggenheim Fellowship. Espada teaches English at the University of Massachusetts-Amherst.

Malaika Favorite received her BFA and MFA in art from LSU. She won the 2016 Broadside Lotus Press Naomi Long Madgett Poetry Award for her collection of poems, *Ascension*, published in 2016 by Broadside Lotus Press. Other publications include: *Dreaming At The Manor* (Finishing Line Press, 2014), and *Illuminated Manuscript*, published by New Orleans Poetry Journal Press, 1991.

Gary Fincke's latest collection is *Bringing Back the Bones: New and Selected Poems* (Stephen F. Austin University Press, 2016). His next collection *The Infinity Room* won the 2018 Wheelbarrow Books/Michigan State University Prize for Established Poets and will be published by MSU early in 2019.

Deborah Ford recently retired from Mississippi Valley State University. She continues to write, lecture, and travel.

Chris Forhan is the author of the memoir *My Father Before Me* as well as three books of poetry: *Black Leapt In*; *The Actual Moon, The Actual Stars;* and *Forgive Us Our Happiness*. He has won a National Endowment for the Arts Fellowship and two Pushcart Prizes. Born and raised in Seattle, he lives in Indianapolis, where he teaches at Butler University. See www.chrisforhan.com.

Maria Mazziotti Gillan is the author of twenty-two books. Her newest poetry collection is *What Blooms in Winter* (NYQ, 2016). She received the American Book Award for *All That Lies Between Us* (Guernica Editions). Professor Gillan is the Founder and Executive Director of the Poetry Center at Passaic County Community College in Paterson, New Jersey and editor of the *Paterson Literary Review*. She is also Director of the Creative Writing Program and Professor of Poetry at SUNY–Binghamton University.

Vicki Graham lives in two places, each with its own gifts, from the pasque flowers of the Minnesota prairie to the spotted sandpipers of Oregon's coastal rivers. Recently retired, she taught for many years at the University of Minnesota, Morris, as a professor of literature, creative writing, and environmental studies. She has published three volumes of poetry, most recently *The Hummingbird's Tongue*, published by Red Dragonfly Press.

William Greenway's newest collection *Selected Poems* was the winner of the 2014 FutureCycle Press Poetry Book of the Year Award. Both his tenth and eleventh collections won Ohio Poetry Book of the Year Awards. He has published in *Poetry, American Poetry Review, Georgia Review, Southern Review, Poetry Northwest, Shenandoah,* and *Prairie Schooner.* He's the Distinguished Professor Emeritus of English at Youngstown State University, but lives now in Ephrata, PA.

Twyla M. Hansen is Nebraska's State Poet, and co-director of *Poetry from the Plains: A Nebraska Perspective* (poetryfromtheplains.org). Her newest book is *Rock • Tree • Bird.* Previous books have twice won the Nebraska Book Award, and one was selected as a Nebraska 150 Notable Book. Her writing is published in *Academy of American Poets, Poetry Out Loud Anthology, Prairie Schooner, Midwest Quarterly, Organization & Environment, Encyclopedia of the Great Plains,* and more.

James Harms is the author of nine books of poetry including *Rowing with Wings,* published by Carnegie Mellon University Press in 2017.

Dixon Hearne's work has been twice nominated for the Pushcart Prize. His latest book is *Plainspeak: New and Selected Poems.* Other work includes Texas Review Press's *Southern Poetry Anthology: Louisiana, Down to the Dark River* from Louisiana Literature Press, *Tulane Review, New Plains Review, Poetry South, Weber: The Contemporary West, Big Muddy,* etc. His website: dixonhearne.com

Kathleen Hellen is the author of the collection *Umberto's Night,* winner of the Jean Feldman Poetry Prize, and two chapbooks, *The Girl Who Loved Mothra* and *Pentimento.* Awards include the Thomas Merton Poetry Prize, as well as prizes from the *H.O.W. Journal* and *Washington Square Review.*

Sister Lou Ella Hickman, I.W.B.S., is a member of the Sisters of the Incarnate Word and Blessed Sacrament. Presently, she is a writer as well as a spiritual director. Her poems and articles have been published in numerous magazines as well as in *After Shocks: Poetry of Recovery for Life-Shattering Events* edited by Tom Lombardo and in *Down to the Dark River* edited by Philip Kolin. Her first book of poetry, *she: robed and wordless,* published by Press 53, was released in the fall of 2017.

Angela Jackson-Brown is a graduate of Spalding University's low-residency in Creative Writing program, and an award-winning author who teaches in the English Department at Ball State University. She is the author of a novel and she has written and directed several plays, including a musical about Robert F. Kennedy entitled *Dear Bobby* that will debut later this spring. Negative Capability Press will also be releasing her poetry collection, *House Repair* in 2018.

Tim Kahl is the author of *Possessing Yourself* (CW Books, 2009), *The Century of Travel* (CW Books, 2012) and *The String of Islands* (Dink, 2015). His work has been published in many magazines in the US and abroad. He is vice president and events coordinator of The Sacramento Poetry Center. He plays flutes, guitars, and ukuleles and currently teaches at California State University, Sacramento, where he sings lieder while walking on campus between classes.

George Kalamaras, former Poet Laureate of Indiana (2014-2016), is the author of fifteen books of poetry, eight of which are full-length, including *Kingdom of Throat-Stuck Luck*, winner of the Elixir Press Poetry Prize (2011). He is Professor of English at Indiana University-Purdue University Fort Wayne, where he has taught since 1990.

David Kirby's collection *The House on Boulevard St.: New and Selected Poems* was a finalist for the National Book Award in 2007. Kirby is the author of *Little Richard: The Birth of Rock 'n' Roll*, which the *Times Literary Supplement* of London called "a hymn of praise to the emancipatory power of nonsense." Kirby's honors include fellowships from the National Endowment of the Arts and the Guggenheim Foundation. His latest poetry collection is *Get Up, Please*.

Brian Jerrold Koester holds an MFA from the Bennington Writing Seminars. He is a *Best of the Net Anthology* nominee. His work has appeared or is forthcoming in *AGNI, HeartWood, The Delmarva Review, Right Hand Pointing, Peacock Journal, Poetry Pacific, Louisiana Literature,* and elsewhere. He lives in Lexington, Massachusetts and has been a freelance cellist.

Philip C. Kolin is the Distinguished Professor of English Emeritus at the University of Southern Mississippi where he is also the Editor Emeritus of the *Southern Quarterly*. He has published more than 40 books, including critical studies of Tennessee Williams, Shakespeare, Edward Albee, Adrienne Kennedy, as well as eight collections of poems, the two most recent being *Emmett Till in Different States: Poems* (Third World, 2015) and *Benedict's Daughter: Poems* (Wipf and Stock, 2017). Kolin has also published a business and technical writing textbook, *Successful Writing at Work*, now in its 11th edition from Cengage Publishing.

Ted Kooser is a former U. S. Poet Laureate and Pulitzer winner. His *Kindest Regards: New and Selected Poems* is soon to be published by Copper Canyon Press, and his fourth picture book for children is in production at Candlewick Press. He lives in rural Nebraska and teaches part time at the University of Nebraska in Lincoln.

Bill Lavender is a poet and novelist living in New Orleans. His seven books have been published by Chax Press, Black Widow, Potes and Poets, and Trembling Pillow. He is the proprietor of Lavender Ink / Diálogos (lavenderink.org) and the co-founder of the New Orleans Poetry Festival.

Sydney Lea, a Pulitzer finalist, was Poet Laureate of Vermont (2011-15). His twelfth collection of poems, *No Doubt the Nameless*, was published in 2016 by Four Way Books. His fourth collection of lyrical essays, *What's the Story? Short Takes on a Life Grown Long*, appeared in 2015 from Green Writers Press. Lea founded and for thirteen years edited the *New England Review*.

Philip L. Levin, M.D., has promoted writers with a regional magazine, anthologies, and writing conferences. His 24 published books include contemporary and historic fictions, a suspense thriller, children photo books, anthologies, fantasy early reader books, and audio books., Over a hundred of his stories, poems, and articles have appeared in print. To support his writing, he's a 40-year veteran of the emergency department.

Michael A. Lofaro is a professor of English at the University of Tennessee. He specializes in the literature of the early American West and serves as the general editor of the scholarly edition of *The Works of James Agee*.

Peter Makuck's sixth volume of poetry, *Mandatory Evacuation* (2016), was published by, BOA Editions, Ltd. Twice winner of the annual Brockman Campbell award for the best book of poetry published by a

North Carolinian, Makuck founded and edited *Tar River Poetry* from 1978 to 2006, the year he retired from East Carolina University as a Distinguished Professor Emeritus.

Paul Mariani is the University Professor of English Emeritus at Boston College. He has published 250 essays and reviews, as well as scholarly chapters in anthologies and encyclopedias, and is the author of 18 books, including seven volumes of poetry, as well as biographies of William Carlos Williams, Berryman, Lowell, Hart Crane, Hopkins, and—most recently—Wallace Stevens (*The Whole Harmonium,* 2016). His most recent book of poems is *Epitaphs for the Journey.*

Tod Marshall is the author of three collections of poetry; his most recent is *Bugle* (Canarium Books, 2014) which won the Washington State Book Award. He teaches at Gonzaga University in Spokane, Washington From 2016-18, he served as the Washington State Poet Laureate.

Karen McPherson is a poet and translator as well as a Professor Emerita of French at the University of Oregon. Her book *Skein of Light* (Airlie Press, 2014) was a finalist for the Eric Hoffer Book Award for Poetry. She is also the author of the chapbook *Sketching Elise* and of a book-length translation into English of essays by Quebec poet Louise Warren. Her work has appeared in numerous literary journals including *Potomac Review, Descant,* and *Beloit Poetry Journal.*

Peter Meinke's latest books are *Lucky Bones* (Pitt Poetry Series), *The Expert Witness* (short stories, U. of Tampa Press), and *To Start With, Feel Fortunate* (essays, winner of the 2017 William Meredith Award). He is Poet Laureate of Florida.

Caryn Mirriam-Goldberg, the 2009-13 Kansas Poet Laureate, is the author of 21 books, including two novels, a non-fiction book on the Holocaust, a bioregional memoir on cancer and community, and six poetry collections. Her recent books are *Miriam's Well,* a novel, and *Everyday Magic,* a memoir. Founder of Transformative Language Arts at Goddard College where she teaches, Mirriam-Goldberg leads writing workshops widely, and with singer Kelley Hunt, writing and singing retreats. www.CarynMirriamGoldberg.com

Robert Morgan is the author of fourteen books of poetry, most recently *Dark Energy*, 2015. He has also published eleven works of fiction, including *Chasing the North Star*, 2016. His volumes of nonfiction include *Boone: A Biography*, 2007. Recipient of awards from the American Academy of Arts and Letters and the Fellowship of Southern Writers, he is Kappa Alpha Professor of English at Cornell University.

Mary Murphy is an English instructor at the University of South Alabama. She has presented her poetry at the New Orleans Poetry Festival, Alabama Book Festival, Library of Congress, and other venues. Her next book of poetry is scheduled for publication in 2019.

Robert Nazarene is founding editor of the *American Journal of Poetry*. In 2006, his imprint published the winning volume for the National Book Critics Award in poetry. He is the author of *Church* (2006) and *Empire de la Mort* (2018.) His work is featured in *AGNI, Callaloo, The Iowa Review, The Journal of The American Medical Association, Plume, Ploughshares, Salmagudi* and elsewhere, including *Hurricane Blues*.

Nick Norwood's poems have appeared widely in such places as *The Paris Review, Oxford American, Shenandoah,* US Poet Laureate Ted Kooser's *American Life in Poetry, The Writer's Almanac with Garrison Keillor, Pushcart Prize XLII*, and elsewhere. His recent collection, *Gravel and Hawk*, won the Hollis Summers Prize. He teaches at Columbus State University, where he directs the Carson McCullers Center for Writers and Musicians in Columbus, GA, and Nyack, NY.

Linda Pastan has published 14 volumes of poetry. Her book, *A Dog Runs Through It,* was published in May of 2018. She has been Poet Laureate of Maryland, and in 2003 won the Ruth Lilly Poetry Prize for lifetime achievement.

Joseph Pearce, who was born and raised in England and now resides in South Carolina, is a Senior Editor at the Augustine Institute, editor of the *St. Austin Review,* series editor of the Ignatius Critical Editions, and author of books on Shakespeare, Oscar Wilde, G. K. Chesterton and J. R. R. Tolkien. His verse tapestry, *Death Comes for the War Poets* (St. Augustine's Press), premiered off Broadway in 2017 to critical acclaim.

Marge Piercy's 19th poetry book, *Made in Detroit* (Knopf), was recently published in paperback, and follows *The Hunger Moon: New & Selected Poems, 1980-2010*. Her 17 published novels include *Sex Wars*; *Dance the Eagle to Sleep* and *Vida*, all reissued by PM Press, as well as *The Cost of Lunch, Etc.*(short stories) and *My Life, My Body* (essays, poems, interview). Her memoir is *Sleeping with Cats* (Harper Perennial). She has given readings, speeches, and workshops at over 500 venues in the US and abroad.

Kevin Rabas, Kansas Poet Laureate (2017-2019), teaches at Emporia State University, where he leads the poetry and playwriting tracks and chairs the Department of English, Modern Languages, and Journalism. He has nine books, including *Lisa's Flying Electric Piano*, a Kansas Notable Book and Nelson Poetry Book Award winner.

Doug Ramspeck is the author of six poetry collections and one collection of short stories. His most recent book, *Black Flowers,* is forthcoming from LSU Press. Individual poems have appeared in *The Kenyon Review*, *The Southern Review*, *Slate*, and *The Georgia Review*. His short story collection, *The Owl That Carries Us Away*, is published by BkMk Press (University of Missouri-Kansas City). He teaches at The Ohio State University at Lima.

Diane Raptosh's fourth book of poetry, *American Amnesiac* (Etruscan Press), was longlisted for the 2013 National Book Award. The recipient of three fellowships in literature from the Idaho Commission on the Arts, she served as Boise Poet Laureate (2013), as well as the Idaho Writer-in-Residence (2013-2016). Raptosh teaches creative writing and runs the program in Prison Studies at The College of Idaho. Her most recent book of poems, *Human Directional*, was published by Etruscan Press in Fall 2016.

Joseph Ross is the author of three books of poetry: *ACHE* (2017), *Gospel of Dust* (2013), and *Meeting Bone Man*, (2012). His poems have appeared in many publications including the *Los Angeles Times, Drumvoices Revue,* and *Poet Lore.* He teaches English and Creative Writing at Gonzaga College High School in Washington, D.C. and writes at JosephRoss.net.

Jason Roush is the author of four books of poetry and is currently working on his fifth collection titled *Elsewhere*. He's also an arts critic for a variety of venues and works at the University of Massachusetts, Boston.

Sonia Sanchez, poet, activist, and scholar, was the Laura Carnell Professor of English and Women's Studies at Temple University. She is the recipient of both the Robert Frost Medal for distinguished lifetime service to American poetry and the Langston Hughes Poetry Award. One of the most important writers of the Black Arts Movement, Sanchez is the author of sixteen books.

Pat Schneider is author of ten books, five of poetry, five of prose. Two are from Oxford University Press: *Writing Alone and With Others* and *How the Light Gets In: Writing as a Spiritual Practice*. She is founder of Amherst Writers & Artists and the AWA Press, which has published 39 books. A new collection of poems, *The Weight of Love,* is forthcoming.

Martha Serpas has published three collections of poetry, *Côte Blanche, The Dirty Side of the Storm,* and *The Diener*. Her work has appeared in *The New Yorker, The Nation,* and *Southwest Review* and has been anthologized in *The Art of the Sonnet* and the *Library of America's American Religious Poems*. Active in efforts to restore Louisiana's wetlands, she co-produced *Veins in the Gulf,* a documentary about coastal erosion. She teaches at the University of Houston and serves as a hospital trauma chaplain.

Marley Stuart is a baker who lives in New Orleans with his wife. A graduate of the Bennington Writing Seminars, his stories and poems have recently appeared or are forthcoming in *The Chattahoochee Review, Permafrost, Xavier Review, L'Éphémère Review, The Rising Phoenix Review, Occulum,* and *About Place*.

Virgil Suárez is the author of eight poetry collections, most recently *90 Miles: Selected and New,* published by the University of Pittsburgh Press. His new book is entitled *Indigo*. When he is not writing, he is out riding his Yamaha V-Star 1100 Classic up and down the Blue Highways of the Southeastern United States.

Mary Swander is the Executive Director of AgArts, a non-profit designed to imagine and promote a healthy food system through the arts. She is also the Artistic Director of Swander Woman Productions, a theatrical touring troupe. With fourteen books, Swander is the Poet Laureate of Iowa, having published widely in poetry, non-fiction, and drama. Her latest book of poetry is T*he Girls on the Roof.* Swander holds dual citizenship in the U.S. and Ireland.

Leonard A. Temme, a native New Yorker, studied poetry with Marie Ponsot, Sue Walker, David Ray, and Walter Spara, and has been writing for years. Following extensive formal training in music composition, he earned a doctorate in neuropsychology. His day job is as a research scientist in a government laboratory. He has two sons and four step children, all of whom are very generous with him.

James Torrens, S.J., has been a teacher of English at Santa Clara University, California; Tuskegee Institute, Alabama; and la Universdad Iberoamericana, Tijuana, Mexico. He was Associate Editor and Poetry Editor at *America Magazine*, 1990-1999. He is a Jesuit priest living at Gonzaga University in Spokane, Washington.

Jacqueline Allen Trimble lives and writes in Montgomery, Alabama, where she is a professor of English and chairs the Department of Languages and Literatures at Alabama State University. A Cave Canem Fellow and a 2017 Alabama State Council on the Arts Literary Fellow, her poetry has appeared in *The Louisville Review, The Offing,* and *Blue Lake Review. American Happiness.* Her first collection was published by NewSouth Books and won the Balcones Poetry Prize.

Sue Brannan Walker is Professor Emerita at the University of South Alabama where she served as Distinguished Professor of Creative Writing and Chair of the Department, Poet Laureate of Alabama from 2003-2012, and publisher / editor of Negative Capability Press. She has published eleven books, the latest from Clemson University Press in 2017.

Shanti Weiland's first book, *Sister Nun,* was the 2015 winner of the Negative Capability Press Book Contest, judged by Amy King. Her second book, *Cracked Planet* is forthcoming from Negative Capability

Press. She currently teaches writing and literature at the University of Alabama; authors the blog, *The Poets That You Meet;* and curates the web corner, *Online Enlightenment.* You can find her at shantiweiland.com.

Carey Scott Wilkerson has authored numerous plays, including *Seven Dreams of Falling* (Black Box Press), two poetry collections, *Threading Stone* (New Plains Press), and edited a poetry anthology *Stone River Sky* (Negative Capability Press), has written three operetta libretti including *Eddie›s Stone Song, Odyssey of the First Pasaquoyan*, and a forthcoming hybrid-form novel, *Ariadne's Knot.* He is an Assistant Professor of Creative Writing at Columbus State University

Jianqing Zheng is the author of *The Landscape of Mind* (Slapering Hol Press), recipient of the Mississippi Arts Commission's Literary Artist Fellowships, and editor of *African American Haiku* and *The Other World of Richard Wright* (University Press of Mississippi). His poetry has appeared in *Tar River, Mississippi Review, Poet Lore, Poetry East*, and *Spillway.* He has edited a collection of essays on Sonia Sanchez which was published in 2017.

www.ingramcontent.com/pod-product-compliance
Lightning Source LLC
Chambersburg PA
CBHW030241170426
43202CB00007B/79